STAND UP AND DELIVER

A nervous rookie on the comedy circuit

Andy Kind

MONARCH
B O O K S

Oxford, UK & Grand Rapids, Michigan, USA

First published in the UK in 2011 by Monarch Books (a publishing imprint of Lion Hudson plc) and by Elevation (a publishing imprint of the Memralife Group):
Lion Hudson plc, Wilkinson House, Jordan Hill Road, Oxford OX2 8DR
Tel: +44 (0)1865 302750; Fax +44 (0)1865 302757;
email monarch@lionhudson.com; www.lionhudson.com
Memralife Group, 14 Horsted Square, Uckfield, East Sussex TN22 1QG
Tel: +44 (0)1825 746530; Fax +44 (0)1825 748899;
www.elevationmusic.com

ISBN 978 0 85721 025 8 (print)
ISBN 978 0 85721 112 5 (ePub)
ISBN 978 0 85721 111 8 (Kindle)
ISBN 978 0 85721 113 2 (PDF)

Distributed by:
UK: Marston Book Services, PO Box 269, Abingdon, Oxon, OX14 4YN

The text paper used in this book has been made from wood independently certified as having come from sustainable forests.

British Library Cataloguing Data
A catalogue record for this book is available from the British Library.

Printed and bound in Great Britain by Clays Ltd, St Ives plc.

This book is dedicated to Doreen Rowley,
from her eldest grandson.

X

If I must boast, I would rather boast about the things that show how weak I am.

2 Corinthians 11:30 (New Living Translation)

Contents

September

Dear Lord…

My first gig came out of the blue.

I was driving to play football with a friend of mine when my mobile rang and flashed up "Unknown Caller".

I don't know about you, but I always get a little bit frightened by that. You'll learn as we go along that I have an overactive imagination, so when I see "Unknown Caller", I just picture a man in a cloak with bony fingers and no face. I have this horrible fear that I'll answer the phone to the grim reaper, he'll simply say "It's time", and I'll slump, lifeless, back into my chair.

This whole series of thoughts was making me very tense, and so I answered the phone like someone opening the front door of a long-abandoned Victorian house.

"H-h-hello?"

"Hi, it's Jane from Mirth Control Comedy. Are you free to do a gig in Bath tonight?"

Realizing I'd managed to stave off Death for another day, I breathed a sigh of relief − until I understood what was actually happening.

I was being offered a chance to do stand-up comedy!

I'd never done it before, and had only just registered on the agency's site as a newbie act looking for gigs. But here I was, being invited to travel down south and actually perform.

The reality of the situation − living in Stoke-on-Trent and on my way to play football − meant I would have to set off straight away, wearing nothing but a football strip and thus leaving my friend Steve to walk the final two miles to the match. I had no choice…

"Yes, I'm free," I replied, hoping that Steve would feel an extended pre-match warm-up might do him some good.

"Great, it's the Cellar Bar in the centre of town. Show starts at 8.30, get there for 8.00 – you'll be on in the middle. Bye…"

The line went dead.

"Steve, there's good news and there's bad news," I said.

Steve is still in my top friends on Facebook and I'm godfather to his son, so I won't tell you what he said – but Gordon Ramsey, had he been there, might well have asked him to tone it down a bit.

"Score a goal for me!" I shouted back to Steve as I drove off, leaving him stranded. The hand gesture he gave me in return suggested that he would try to score two.

As I hit the M6 south at Junction 15 and the road to Bath stretched out in front of me, I remember thinking something quite profound that has stuck with me ever since:

"This is the worst idea anyone has ever had!"

But I was on my way. I was finally pursuing my lifelong dream and, though I didn't know it at the time, a new career was about to start. I stopped at Stafford services to buy a pack of mini pork-pies and ring my Mum, to tell her the news. My Mum has an acute gift for the profound, fully equal to my own, and when I told her about this momentous occasion, she replied, "Oh, if I'd known in advance I could have done you a packed lunch!"

Rock and roll.

The moment I passed the Cellar Bar in Bath, my legs turned comprehensively to jelly. As I exited my car, shaking with fear, I must have looked like some hideous ventriloquist's dummy that had sprung to life and turned on his master.

I'd spent most of the journey trying to remember some of the jokes I'd written over the previous few weeks, after I'd had the initial crazy idea to "hit the boards". On the phone, Jane had asked me to do five minutes, but I'd never timed myself and so had no idea whether I had too much or not enough material. More than that, I had no idea whether anything I'd written was in any way funny. In a moment of grotesque clarity, I longed for the Reaperman to call for a catch-up – or at least send a text, if he was trying to keep billing costs down.

Walking into the Porter Cellar Bar and down the flight of steps to the comedy club, I shuffled past the healthy line of punters waiting to pay to get in. A woman with a cash box accosted me. "Can I help?" she asked.

In reply, I asserted something that, over 600 gigs later, still feels a bit odd and a bit beautiful:

"I'm one of the comedians."

I felt like a complete fraud saying it, reminiscent of that scene in *The Great Escape* where Richard Attenborough bluffs his way onto the bus past the Nazi officer by pretending to be French. I was half expecting to be shown through, and the woman would say "Good luck", I'd say "Thank you", we'd both display looks of dawning realization and panic, after which I'd be chased through the streets of Bath and eventually shot as I tried to cross some train tracks.

Bizarrely, she bought my story, affirmed they were expecting me and showed me through into the bar.

The show started and I sat through the compère and opening act, thinking how good they were, how confident they looked and how loose my rectal muscles felt. That is one of the drawbacks with comedy: the terror. No matter how good you get, nor how many gigs you perform at, from the moment you arrive at a venue until you go on, you constantly need the toilet (or at least I do). I was experiencing this now for the first time, and I couldn't honestly say at that moment what was scaring me more: the thought of the crowd not laughing, or the thought of the crowd laughing a lot as I went on and, instead of telling jokes, just stood there transfixed

9

by the light and retaining zero control over my bowels.

Before I knew it, the show had rocketed into its first break of the evening, which meant one thing: I was next.

I went into the Green Room where all the other acts were dissecting the first section of the show. Ninia Benjamin had opened the proceedings and had gone down a storm. She was scrutinizing a piece of paper, using a biro to tick off certain words – presumably symbolizing bits of new material she had road-tested. Also present were a double-act called Electric Forecast (or Big Cook, Little Cook if you are of the CBeebies persuasion). Unaware that this was my first gig, they were asking me questions like, "Who's your agent?" and "You got any TV projects on the go?"

"Well, not really. I'm trying to work my way through every episode of *Friends* in a week, but apart from that..."

I tried to chat politely, but amidst all the happy banter, rib-tickling and general joviality, I had never felt more lonely or quite as stranded.

Everyone else in the club seemed completely at ease with their role for the evening. The barman knew how to pour pints; the audience knew how to sit down and watch what was in front of them; the other comedians knew how to say something funny and wait for a roar of laughter to come rolling back. It had all happened before and would all happen again. But not for me. I was a virgin, a newbie, a rookie: an island of panic in a sea of certainty and self-assurance.

The fifteen-minute break ended. The crowd excitedly retook their seats, a strong scent of beer and wine now filling the underground space. The venue, being subterranean, had a dank clamminess to it that emanated from the walls and tickled my throat. It reminded me of visiting Smuggler's Cove in Newquay as a child.

I wish I was there now.

The other acts went "out front" to watch the show, while the compère, Sally-Anne Hayward, waited for the soundman to play the *A-Team* theme so she could retake the stage.

"I'll just do about five at the top, then bring you straight on. Is that cool?"

"Sure."

"Have a good 'un!" She winked at me, I heard the sound of machine-gun fire as the theme tune kicked in and she was back on stage, leaving me alone in the Green Room.

Apparently, if you have a problem and no one else can help, you can hire the A-Team.

Well, yes, I have a problem – I'm about to humiliate myself in front of 100 people. Where's Hannibal now?!

Please, B.A., for all the times I watched you do it as a boy, please drive a van through this wall now and get me to the Mexican border – I'll make it on my own from there.

In those five or so minutes before my first ever foray onto a stage, I called out to God more plaintively than perhaps I've ever done since. Over the previous weeks, I'd felt a strong calling to give comedy a go. I'd flirted with it, wrestled with it, dismissed it, laughed it off, but I couldn't shake the feeling that this was what God wanted for my life.

Well, God, if this is right, it's time for you to prove it to me. I've failed at so much – please don't let me mess this up. Help me, Lord…

"Ladies and Gentleman, please welcome to the stage, Mr Andy Kind!!!!…"

I stepped into the light.

It's curious, the minutiae you remember from key moments in your life. I can't remember all the material I used that night. Nor can I remember what I was wearing as I stepped from the safety of the Green Room out onto the modest stage. But I do remember that a man in the front row looked like Moira Stewart, and that the woman with him wore a crimson shawl over her right shoulder.

And I remember the lights. If I close my eyes, I can still feel the glare of the spots as they bored into me, exposing me to an expectant room and causing me to squint instinctively.

I never factored that in when I rehearsed my flimsy set in front of the bedroom mirror. You don't. You think it's simply going to be a case of deliver punch line, wait for laugh.

But those lights burned. They burned and disorientated, leaving me more paralysed than a rabbit facing down a juggernaut. And then there was the perspiration. I may not remember the clothes I was wearing, but I do recall the moist patches under my arms, and the way they spread rapidly like a sweaty Genghis Khan.

I remember all of that. And I remember being really scared – scared that this was all a huge mistake. My mouth was drier than Jack Dee's act, and my attempt at "Hello, how're you doing?" got lost somewhere between the larynx and the teeth.

But most of all, I remember saying: "Every weekend, my Dad dresses as a clown for children's parties. It would be more acceptable if anyone had asked him to." Then I remember a short, deep silence where time seemed to slow right down and my hopes and dreams congregated like *Big Brother* contestants on eviction night.

And then, if I remember rightly, they laughed.

It was brilliant!

After all the worry leading up to the gig, it seems wonderfully simple in retrospect: I went on stage, started talking, and people laughed (at my jokes – not because I have a ridiculous voice or anything).

It may entirely undermine the concept of writing a book about doing stand-up, but I can't describe in words the sensation I felt when I got that first laugh; or when I left the stage at the end to a big, appreciative cheer. It was an experience that seemed to wrench me out of my past, dull existence and bring me hurtling into the visceral present – like *Quantum Leap*, but in reverse... and without the blue light… or the lecherous hologram. It was nothing like *Quantum Leap*.

The journey back from Bath took two hours but seemed to fly by in an instant. At the time, I'd been out of work for several months and my levels of self-esteem had been languishing around gutter level, with a view to going subterranean. And yet, in the space of five minutes on stage, my sense of self-worth seemed to pick itself up, dust itself off, spontaneously grow a pair of wings and shoot upwards into the ether. I felt invincible. Even my satnav, Debbie, seemed to be issuing directions with a sense of reverence and awe:

"At the roundabout, do what you like, you legend!"

I didn't get a wink of sleep that night. I just ended up re-running the gig over and over in my mind, pulsing with the joy of seeing all those happy faces who had laughed at my jokes – at *my* jokes! There was no feeling like it.

I couldn't wait for the morning to come so I could tell everyone about it. After years of searching, I had finally found the thing in life I was best at.

When morning dawned, I started systematically ringing everyone in my phone book. On the one hand, my friends seemed delighted; on the other, ABC Taxis and Domino's Pizza seemed a little confused, while the Speaking Clock came across as, at best, ambivalent.

I just couldn't get my head around how well it had gone. To put it into some kind of context, the last time I'd spoken in front of an audience, nobody had listened and someone threw a bottle of beer at me. In fairness, family Christmases are always a challenge.

My Mum was the most pleased to hear about the gig, bless her. I imagine the thought of her first-born not being a complete calamity in everything he attempts must have provided some comfort.

Dad was also pleased that it had gone well, but rained on the parade slightly by asking, "How much did it pay?"

"Well, nothing. It was an open-spot."

"Wouldn't you be better served looking for work, then?"

Whilst Dad's pragmatism was like getting a vial of acid in the face, he did make a valid point. All this post-gig adrenaline and self-aggrandizement was fine, but what did it actually mean? I had no idea what to do next. In my ignorance, I'd half-expected to come off stage and be met by a mêlée of talent scouts, dancing girls and gift-bearing elves. In reality, I was met by a mad bloke in his fifties who mistook me for his old Geography teacher. It was hardly a Hollywood fairytale.

So what was I supposed to do now? With a jolt of reality, it dawned on me that, actually, nothing had changed. I'd done one gig which, to be fair, had been a success, but to what avail? Max Clifford wasn't on the phone offering his patronage; Jonathan Ross hadn't popped round to give me a guest slot on his *Friday Night* show. Even the gift-bearing elves hadn't as yet materialized.

There is a huge public misconception about stand-up comedy. A lot of people seem to presume that top comedians – Billy Connolly, Frank Skinner, Lee Evans etc. – just appear on TV, and that, outside the small screen, stand-up doesn't really exist. It's that idea that one day Peter Kay was sitting with his mates in a pub, reducing them to tears with his "It's funny 'cos it's true" style of humour, when a talent scout shuffled up to him at the bar and said, "I like the look of you, son. I'm booking for a show at the Hammersmith Apollo next month – fancy coming along and doing an hour?"

That is not the reality. The reality – as we will find out together – is that making your mates laugh doesn't make you a comedian. Doing one good gig in a pub doesn't make you a comedian. Greasing yourself up and pouting like a girl doesn't make you Cristiano Ronaldo. On all counts, there's more to it than that.

Fearing that the comedy endeavour might be nothing more than a storm in a teacup, I scoured Google for "comedy nights in the Midlands". Google had obviously been chatting to my Dad and flashed up "Did you mean Jobs in the Midlands?"

"Don't make me switch to Alta Vista," I retorted.

After a good hour of surfing, I managed to collate a small batch of phone numbers and set about systematically calling them – without much luck. Either the numbers were no longer in use or I was barking up the wrong tree:

"Sorry, mate, we did have a comedy night, but that closed down 100 years ago."

"Yeah, you're way out of your depth, mate – we only book professional acts. Are you making a living as a comic?"

"We do insist that all our comedians are signed-up members of the BNP. Are you making a living as a racist?"

As luck would have it – and just as I was wondering whether I'd ever get the chance to perform for a second time – I stumbled across an advert in *The Sentinel*, Stoke-on-Trent's local paper: "Ribbed Comedy night. Thursday, 8pm. Fat Cat Bar. Come and see some of the North-West's top comedy talent."

I need to be at that night, I decided. I rang Steve and suggested he tag along. Still smarting from being dumped at the side of an A-road a couple of days before, my friend agreed, but on the proviso that he could bring a video camera so that, if it was a disaster, he could claim £250 from *You've Been Framed*.

***

I'd never heard of a comedy night in Stoke before. As much as I love my home town, we're one of those cities where, culturally, not a lot happens. Subsequently, when something exciting does come along, we milk it. In 2005, London was given the Olympics, and there were all those celebrations in Trafalgar Square – fireworks, flag-waving, people hugging and kissing in the fountain. That's how we reacted in Stoke when it was announced we were getting a Matalan.

"Put it next to the Primark – our dream will be complete!"

I wasn't on the bill for the evening, so I just hoped to turn up, enjoy the comedy and get some tips from the guy running the show. During the first interval, I approached the bloke who looked most like he was in charge and introduced myself.

"Oh, I heard about that gig you did down in Bath!" he didn't say. Instead, he couldn't get my name right.

"Andy Cline, did you say?"

"No, Andy Kind."

"Hind?"

This went on for about half a minute, before I actually got round to asking him about how I could get more gigs.

"You're after more gigs, are you?"

"That's right!"

"Well, Anthony… as it happens, the guy who was due to be on next is stuck in traffic and has rung to say he's pulling out. Do you want to go on now?"

A shiver ran down my spine, like when you're at school and some joker puts an ice cube down your back. *Go on now?* I didn't feel ready; I hadn't gone over any of my stuff since Bath; I was annoyed at being called Anthony.

"Sure, I'd love to go on now," I replied.

"Great. I'll do five at the top, then bring you straight on. Have a good 'un."

I went back to Steve, completely unaware that several years later I'd look back on the "ice-cube down your back" analogy and find it completely inadequate. Once again, the bitter-sweet mix of adrenaline and utter terror washed over me. Hastily, I tried to recall my set-list from the previous gig. Steve put new film in the camera.

There were fewer people in Fat Cat's than at the Cellar bar – about fifty – but somehow that made it more frightening, more personal. Also, this was my home town. What if it went badly and everyone got to hear about it?

What if, for weeks after, old ladies and little children alike see me in the street, start pointing and making clown noises? What if ABC Taxis ring me up tomorrow and say, "We heard about last night. Don't even think about getting in one of our cabs again, you great loser! And don't think about ordering Domino's either – we've passed on the message. You're a disgrace to the whole of North Staffordshire."

The promoter – who was also compèring – re-started the night, got everyone settled and announced:

"We have a young lad now who's never done comedy before. He might be good, he might be useless. Either way, try not to expect too much. Ladies and gentlemen, please welcome to the stage, Adrian Cline…"

They say a prophet is never accepted in his own town. That might well be true, but I don't know anyone from Stoke called Adrian Cline, and I flipping ripped it!

Moments after I came off stage, dripping with sweat and slightly shell-shocked, the promoter, Wayne, approached me, called me Alistair, and then told me he thought my set was "cracking" and that he had another gig in Crewe I could do. "Now that I've seen you and know you're not crap, I can pass you the details of some other promoters in the North as well."

"Cheers – that would be great."

"You remind me of a young Simon Bligh," he continued. I wasn't sure who he was referring to at the time, but I found out about six months later that Simon Bligh is a top comedian, not a sex offender. Bonus!

The best moment of all came as I was standing at the bar shortly after my set. A young lady approached me and said she thought

I was "funny and very cool". I looked around and there was no sign of hidden cameras or Jeremy Beadle, so I presumed she was serious.

How about that?! I get into comedy and suddenly girls start referring to me as "very cool".

She was mistaken, of course. The man she was speaking to was twenty-four years old, didn't smoke or take drugs, lived with his Mum and Dad and was a born-again Christian. Lock up your daughters!

Anyway, her name was Helen, she was a student at Staffs Uni and she was very pretty. Feeling a bit cocky, I asked her out for coffee and she said "yes". I almost ruined it by forcing her to wait with me so I could check she hadn't given me the number for Flirt-Divert, but she hadn't and we arranged a date.

Comedy, it seemed, was working out a treat. I hadn't felt this excited since I heard Stoke was getting a Matalan.

***

Before I continue telling you about *how* I got into comedy, it might be a good idea to talk about *why* I wanted to in the first place. Equally, it might not be – but it's my book and I play by my own rules.

So, why would I – *why would anyone* – want to become a comedian? Well, it's a good question and I'm glad you asked it. Certainly, it's the main question we have to field in this line of work and something people have probed me on countless times. In general, I think comedians welcome the enquiry – unless it's thrown at us in an over-the-shoulder, "That cost me £5 and my kids need new shoes, you beast" kind of way as someone storms out of a venue.

Every comedian has a different reason for wanting to "tread the boards" (which, incidentally, is a phrase that – until now – hasn't been used since the First World War). Some folks use comedy as a platform for venting their anger and frustration at a world they don't understand; others use it as a way of overturning childhood suffering. Some – though not many – do it primarily as a way of meeting girls – or boys, if you're a lady/homosexual.

Personally, I just love the sound of laughter.

I remember being about seven years old. I loved being that age! It's that time in life where, in the eyes of your parents, the worst thing you could do was to stay inside on a hot day. It was the only thing that really got me told off. Mum would come into the living-room, angrily turn off *Ghostbusters*, open the curtains I'd strategically closed to shield the screen, and order me to go outside and play Cowboys and Indians.

"Woe betide you if I find you inside again! It's a lovely day, now go and play on the swings or I will lose my temper! *Don't make me buy you an ice-cream!!*"

Why couldn't that happen now? Why do only children get reprimanded for not having fun and enjoying creation? Above all things, why shouldn't not enjoying the world be the thing we are scolded for? Wouldn't it be brilliant if you worked in a boring office job and one day your boss stormed in and said, "What the hell are you guys doing?! The sun's out, so's the paddling pool: forget spreadsheets – let's build a den!"

That would be a much better world: a world where games took priority over anything work-related.

"Excuse me, Mr Chief Executive. The Board of Directors want to have a meeting with you this morning. Can I set it up?"

"Let me see… No, I'm afraid not. I'm playing Kiss-Chase this morning. I can fit them in at 2 p.m., just before British Bulldog."

I used to love playing Cowboys and Indians as a child. Myself and a few friends would gather round a John Wayne film, then trek into the fields behind the house to recreate the scenario.

I was quite ignorant as a child. I also needed to be the centre

19

of attention – that's not a good combination. So we'd race into the woods and I'd say, "Right, Cowboys and Indians – I'll be the Cowboy!"

And my mate would say, "Can't I be the Cowboy today?"

To which I'd reply, "Look, Sanjeev, we've been through this…"[1]

Anyway, I digress – sorry. I remember being about seven years old and having a day off school, ill. This was before the days of Sky+ and all that jazz, and so my only means of entertainment was a stack of my Dad's *Blackadder* and *Fawlty Towers* videos. Intrigued by "grown-ups' comedy", I put one on. By the time I returned to school a couple of days later, I'd watched them all right the way through. Twice.

From that point, I think it's fair to say that, over time, I started to develop a sense of what a joke was and how it was possible to use words to make people laugh. Up until then, "comedy" had been all about falling in mud or doing a massive trump. An awakening had taken place, and I had classic British sitcom to thank.

To this day, when asked who my comedy idols are, I always say, "John Cleese, Rowan Atkinson and Steven Woods." (Steven Woods was in my class at school. One time I saw him slip in some mud, the shock of which caused him to let out a massive trump. It was genius.)

Growing up from that point, then, I always wanted to be a comedian. Other children in my class wanted to be footballers or ballet dancers or full-time housewives. (It was an all-boys school, so that seemed a bit weird.)

I got to the age of eighteen and realized that, realistically, hardly anyone does comedy for a living and it was never going to happen for me. Somewhat deflated and underwhelmed, I chose to study French at Warwick University, in the hope that I might grow to

---

1   Irony and a knowing smile don't always translate in written form, but they are very much present in that joke.

love the idea of teaching or translation work. I never did.

Like most students, I frittered my time and abilities away, chasing after self-gratification above any kind of genuine fulfilment. My clean-cut image of today is somewhat at odds with my past. At university I wanted to do three things: sleep with women, get really drunk and form a Spandau Ballet tribute act. As you can imagine, I only ever did two of those things – but as a tribute act, we were fantastic… even when we were hammered.

I was never going to be able to capture a high-flying job in Modern Languages – the reason being, I can't do a French accent.

A supreme example of this occurred during my year abroad in France. Now, the best thing that can happen to you as a language student is that you get mistaken for a native, your ability to speak the language being so high. I was in a shop once (or *un magasin*, to give you the French. Oh yeah, I got a 2:2). I was chatting away in French to the guy behind the counter, when after a while he said, "So tell me, what part of France are you from?"

And I got really excited, because as I've mentioned, my French accent is abysmal. And I really became quite smug, replying, "Sorry, Monsieur, I'm actually English – did you not know that?"

"*Non, non,*" he replied. "I thought you were French… but maybe a bit retarded."

Bizarrely, it wasn't until about a year after I left University that I woke up to the stark fact that making people laugh was my heart's desire – nothing more or less. It didn't matter that it wasn't realistic, or that it flouted my sense of duty to my education. I had an itch that needed scratching and I wouldn't be happy until I'd got my nails into it.

The day after the gig in Stoke, I spoke to Wayne the promoter and he passed me the details for some comedy clubs around the North-West. I made some phone calls, sent off some emails, released a few carrier pigeons, and a couple of days later my diary was scribbled with the details of upcoming gigs. None of them were paid, of course. That's par for the course when you start out, and why a lot of people seeking to earn a quick buck out of stand-up never do more than a couple of gigs.

"But if you're good, we'll have a look at getting you back in a few months for some paid work," was the standard motif.

I was already learning the most valuable lesson you need as a budding stand-up comedian: you have to really want it.

As October approached, I was sure that I did want it; that I could do it; that I would do it. By the end of October, my mentality would change completely, but for now at least I felt assured. I awaited with anticipation my next gig, at a bespoke comedy club I'd never heard of in Manchester: The Frog and Bucket.

October

Autumn had fallen hard over North Staffordshire. The lush verdancy of summer had been replaced by a haunting Stranglers song. Scarves were unfolded from drawers as the first chill permeated the air, and every morning outside my parents' house, uniformed kids trudged mournfully back to school. We all recognize that sinking feeling of going back after a magical summer, and so, as a bona fide adult recently out of full-time education, I did what anyone else would do: I stood at the front door and laughed and pointed.

It was the second Monday of the month, and my diary informed me that people across the world were celebrating Columbus Day. I don't have time to Wikipedia stuff like that, but I presume it involves everyone donning long overcoats and impersonating Peter Faulk.

It may have been the season of decay outside, but inside it felt more like the season of rebirth. I had a new purpose, a renewed passion and, hopefully, a new career was springing.
  "I'm off to a gig now, Dad."
  "You getting paid for it?"
  "… See you later, then."

***

The Frog and Bucket, or "The Frog" as it is affectionately known, is a purpose-built comedy venue in the heart of Manchester. I've played there many times, but the first time is the one I remember. To this day, I always feel a shiver of apprehension as I pass through the front doors and see the stage where so many new comics have started their flight up into the comedy stratosphere – and where so many others have slipped down into the bowels of comedy oblivion, never to return.

I think – and in many cases know – that for any act playing there as an open-spot, no matter how good or experienced you become, there is always something about the Frog – a certain buzz – that makes you feel "brand new" again, and not in a good way.

As I entered the club and felt this buzz for the first time, I was instantly met with a wave of energy from all the students crammed into the place. It was like gatecrashing *Hollyoaks* auditions, ten minutes after the producer had announced, "You've all got the part and it's a free bar!"

The two September gigs had been reasonably well attended, but nothing like this – the place was absolutely rammed. I swallowed hard.

This is a lot of people to do badly in front of…

I'd felt fairly comfortable on the drive up. After all, my first two attempts at being funny had been successful. (No matter how you look at it, that's a 100 per cent hit-rate.) I had asked Steve if he wanted to come along again, but he said his brother was coming round and so he couldn't. When I pointed out that he didn't have a brother, he just put the phone down.

I had passed the sixty minutes it took to get into central Manchester by running through my "new" set-list. A couple of jokes had failed to receive anything more than titters in either Bath or Stoke, and so I handed them their P45s and wished them the best of luck in finding more work. One of them went as follows:

"There are so many skinheads in Stoke-on-Trent, it's like a massive alopecia convention."

Not so much a joke, perhaps, as a morally ambiguous observation – but that's the way it goes. A comedy set requires an evolutionist approach rather than a creationist one. It takes years for all the comedy molecules to form into something that you're truly happy with, and that truly reflects your stance on life. When you first start out as a stand-up, five minutes seems like an eternity to be funny for, and so you include in your set anything that even vaguely resembles a joke. You try it all out on stage, and natural selection takes over. An audience is a great mechanism for the survival of the funniest.

My set, at this stage, was largely comprised of puns and one-liners. You tend to write the sort of stuff that you enjoy watching, and I'd been glued to a Tim Vine DVD for a few months, as well as browsing through various Emo Phillips clips on YouTube. I'd written a few perky one-liners over the previous few days, and had offered them short-term contracts.

But by the time I'd driven past the University, the Aquatic Centre, the Palace Theatre and had parked up amid the towering office buildings, my confidence had waned somewhat and I had started to feel very small. I suddenly felt like I was trespassing somehow. Who was I to come to the home of Northern Soul, The Busby Babes and Steve Coogan, and dare to impose on them with my jokes? What did I have to offer this great city?

I still think there is something daunting about gigs in historic cities – where it is possible to feel submerged by a tide culture. (This is why it's so nice to gig in Milton Keynes, where you know, no matter how badly you do, you'll still be more popular than a roundabout.)

Stepping through the front doors of the Frog and Bucket only served to exacerbate this feeling. This was a *proper* club, purpose-built and designed solely for the task of putting on comedy. On the walls were pictures of the people who'd played there over the years: Johnny Vegas, Dave Spikey and Jason Manford amongst others; all smiling, all happy. These were the guys who had been in my position, done their time in the trenches and broken through into the big time.

Do well here tonight, and that could be you in a year or two…

Do badly, and Cristiano Ronaldo won't be your only reason for hating Manchester…

I was performing as part of a gong-show-style competition for new acts called "Beat The Frog". (Legend doesn't have it that the name came from an incident in 1812, when a group of French scholars were set upon by the bouncers.)

The night still runs, and is a fantastic breeding-ground for flourishing Northern talent. The show is split into two defined sections. In the first section, two "more established" comedians come on and do eight minutes each of tried and tested material to warm up the crowd. There is then a break, in which all the students in the place are actively encouraged to get absolutely ratted on cheap bottles of beer – after which the real fun starts.

Post-break, the compère hands out three cards to random members of the audience. The competition itself consists of between eight and ten open-spots taking the stage one after another and trying to get through five minutes of material without breaking down in tears or being carded off by the paralytic audience. This is made harder by the fact that 80 per cent of all University students these days claim to have ADHD.[2]

An open-spot, by the way, has two definitions. It can either refer to the unpaid middle section of some comedy nights (e.g. Russell Howard is headlining; I'm doing the open-spot). Or, it can be used to define what sort of standard a comedian is at (e.g. "Don't offer him paid work – he's only an open-spot").

So, if, by some miracle, the audience doesn't get bored of an act within the given time-frame, the five-minute marker is announced

---

2   Incidentally, ADHD are the required grades you need to get into Coventry Uni… well, without the A.

by Paul McCartney's "Frog Chorus" being played over the speakers. The act then leaves the stage to appreciative applause and makes a mental note to add the card-holders on Facebook.

The more common scenario, however, is that within about ninety seconds, one of the three card-holders will think something along the lines of, "Whilst I've paid absolutely nothing to get into this night of comedy, this new comedian on stage isn't as good as the professional comedians I've seen on TV. I could be back in halls, watching *Gilmore Girls*. He should be ashamed of himself, coming on stage and trying to entertain me. It is, therefore, only fair to put up my card and shout 'Off, off, off!' as a sign of protest, and encourage others to do the same."

After all three cards have been similarly raised, the compère honks a massive horn and the poor comic is forced to trudge off the stage, while Beck's "I'm a Loser" reverberates around the room – much to the delight of the baying students. The defeated comic then makes a mental note to release a live tiger into the homes of the card-holders.

You can always tell who the new acts are at The Frog. Each "competitor" is given two free drinks tokens as they enter, and within three minutes you can find them standing in the corner of the room, looking sheepish and clutching two bottles of beer. I've always wondered whether the drinks token idea was intended as a homing device for the young newbies who, on turning up at a big venue, scared and unaccompanied, are at least able to scout out other lambs ready for slaughter.

I was one such lamb on this occasion. I'm sure I cut a pretty lonely figure as I stood in the corner of the club, sipping repeatedly from a bottle of Carlsberg. What made things worse was that I thought wearing a T-shirt with the slogan "I'm with stupid" would convey a sense of joviality. I didn't see a flaw until a passing punter pointed out that I was standing next to a mirror.

Crouching isolated in the corner, it reminded me of going on the French exchange in third year, when you arrive at a school in the middle of nowhere and wait for your designated family to come and pick you up – although on this occasion, I wasn't approached by a man with a massive handlebar moustache and told in broken English that I looked fatter in real life.

I was, however, approached by a skinny man with spiky black hair and a quizzical look on his face.

"Are you on tonight?" he asked, contorting his features.

"Yeah, first time."

"Good. I'm on as well. I'm Victor."

"Hi, Victor. I'm Andy Kind."

"Oh, right. Well, I've not heard of you, so I'll assume for now that I'm better."

And so I met Victor Smithers – one of the most ridiculous men I've ever met, and one of my favourite people on this earth.

Looking like the love-child of Sonic the Hedgehog and the Childcatcher from *Chitty Chitty Bang Bang*, Victor is, these days, a very funny, well-respected and well-liked comedian. This hasn't always been the case, though. When I first met him at that early gig, he was already six months into his stand-up career and was already making a name for himself. And that name was "knobhead". It wasn't that people disliked him, you understand; it was more that they wanted him to get hit by a train.

Like any new comic, Victor wanted to get recognition – both on stage from the crowds, and off stage from fellow comics. Most of the new acts I've met in my time have tried to cross that bridge by working hard to write good jokes, and by being polite to their co-workers. This moderate and sagacious approach perhaps seemed a little too formulaic for Victor, who, from the very first time I met him, has referred to himself as "The Legend". So Victor's approach to garnering respect and recognition led to him, in those early days, schooling himself into a perpetual state of social banter, whereby anything that anyone said to him in conversation would instantly be held up to his comedic scrutiny, shredded to pieces and left in a pulpy, blubbering mess on the floor. The intent was always to make him look triumphantly comical to his peers and attractive to any women in the room, but would, instead, often leave people fantasizing about a triumvirate of Victor, an anchor, and the Manchester ship canal.

Years later, he and I were at a gig where we found ourselves chatting at the bar to a group of young ladies that Victor had his eye on.[3] One of them ordered a glass of water from the bar, to which Victor erupted: "Water?! Water?!!! You're in a bar, love. Don't be so boring – live a little."

The young lady replied, "I'm drinking water so I can drive to see my Mum in the hospital after the gig. She's critically ill but she wanted me to come and cheer myself up with some comedy."

"................" Victor responded.

"........................" I added.

Then we left.

So this is the Victor we are meeting now: a man on a permanent charm offensive, where the word "charm" has been Tippexed out and the word "offensive" underlined and highlighted.

"I'll give you some advice," said Victor. "Nobody does well on their first attempt at the Frog. I was an exception to that rule, but I've been told I'm the Future of stand-up, so there you go. Anyway, I'm doing the opening eight minutes tonight. Watch what I do, and try to learn for next time – there's a good lad. Just passing on my experience."

"Have you done this gig lots, then?"

"Yes, twice. And I won it, obviously."

"Both times? That's great."

"Not both times, no. I won it once, and to be fair I would have won it the other time, but I was cheated out of it by four other

---

3   This applies to all young ladies.

comedians, who were funnier and got better responses. Anyway, I'm off for a poo now. You're welcome to come, but it will mean the end of our friendship."

"I'll probably just wait here."

"Very wise. Have a good 'un."

I didn't speak to Victor again that night. He left the club as abruptly as he'd left our conversation, after dying one of the worst deaths I've ever seen. He was so bad, I wondered for a time whether he'd been joking about being the Future of comedy – though I subsequently learned that he was – and still is – deadly serious about that. I think it's fair to say that I liked Victor Smithers from the start, and of all the people I've met in comedy, he is by far my favourite. You will learn later, also, that there is more to him than meets the eye. (NB: He isn't a Transformer. I should clarify that, in case you start building up your hopes that he will suddenly turn into a fighter jet. He won't.)

There was one moment in particular which enamoured him to me. Part way through his set, a voice from the back of the room shouted at him to "Get off!" Victor, bless him, looked absolutely devastated, but from somewhere found the courage to respond with one of the best put-downs I've witnessed.

"Get off? That's not a very good heckle. You should know, sir, never to end a sentence with a preposition."

This brought spontaneous applause from the assembled crowd, and for a moment it looked like Smithers would turn it round. But then, heart-breakingly, the disembodied voice came back with, "All right, then. Get off – now!" An even bigger round of applause erupted, and Victor mumbled, "OK," and sloped off.

As for myself, I'd been drawn to go on at the start of the competition's second half. Neither of the eight-minute acts had done well, and all four of the "froggers" before me had been carded off within three minutes – one of them after only seven seconds because he'd downed both his bottles of beer and accidentally burped whilst saying "Hello." Another act got "croaked" in under two minutes for doing a rather drawn-out and socially inadmissible impression of the footballer, Emmanuel Adebayor. The cards were shooting up with vigour and prompt regularity.

I was not enjoying it at all. I realized with a shudder that this would be my first time in front of a "tough crowd". In Somerset and Staffordshire, everyone had been "up for it" – and there had been other, experienced acts on the bill to deliver the goods.

To make any audience laugh deserves credit, but when they've already been warmed up by professional acts, when they've bought into the spirit of the night, laughed heartily and been given their money's worth, an audience tends to relax more and laugh more readily. But this night had been a complete car-crash of a gig. Everyone except the compère had done badly, and the herd of student cattle was getting more drunk and less tolerant by the minute. With each comedian that went to face them, the young, attractive, well-groomed crowd morphed evermore into a comedy firing squad.

As I stood at the side of the stage, waiting to be riddled with heckle-shaped bullets and wishing I'd placed a cigarillo case in my top pocket, the compère for the night, Toby Hadoke – the only bright spark in the gloom – kicked off the second half, bizarrely, by complimenting the audience. He told them they were responsible for creating the future stars of comedy; that simply by being there, they were helping to hone and sharpen the young guns of the comedy scene. He told them how privileged they were to be seeing a part of the creative process for free, and that they should be proud of themselves.

It was a bold move to try to play mind-games with a loud and bolshy audience, but risks like that are what being a top compère is all about – and Toby is one of the best. The crowd called his bluff, and when he announced "our next act, Andy Kind", in an unspoken act of unity and self-congratulation, a genuine cheer broke out from the gathered mass. The atmosphere had shifted in seconds from a state of out-and-out war to an abrupt ceasefire. Toby had somehow negotiated peace talks, and now I was comedy's ambassador, striding onto stage like an olive branch in a poorly chosen T-shirt.

Just be confident. Don't introduce yourself – just go straight into it.

"Every weekend, my Dad dresses as a clown for children's birthday parties. It would be more acceptable if anyone had asked him to."

There was a pause while all of the booze-soaked brains processed my words. Had I ruined it? After all Toby's work, had I broken the ceasefire by firing a dud onto enemy ground? Had I accidentally napalmed the audience in the face?

Then the laugh came. Not a massive laugh. Not a rolling, rippling laugh that bounces off the walls and takes ages to die down. But a laugh nevertheless, and one that the show needed. Suddenly the tension broke and for the first time that evening there seemed to be a genuine sense of trust in the room.

"Anyway, my name's Andy – hello." I managed to say this without belching. It was simple yet effective.

The rest of my set flew by. I didn't rip it, or storm it, or take the roof off. A couple of my jokes didn't get laughs at all, and one particular short-term contract would need to be revoked. But I got through it and I did the job, and on five minutes Colin the soundman pressed his autocue button and "The Frog Chorus" boomed out into the club. I'd come as a peace envoy, and left unscathed. I'd beaten the Frog.

It paved the way for the remaining comics to also beat the Frog, each of them garnering increased levels of laughter by using the preceding comedian as a slipstream.

At the end of each show, all the successful froggers go into a "clap off", where the audience choose their favourite act of the night. I finished fourth out of eight, which was hardly an historic victory, but several people afterwards credited me with turning the tide of the evening – and only one of those was wearing a T-shirt with the slogan "I'm with stupid". So it wasn't a storming success, but as I once said after beating my partially sighted cousin at table-tennis, a win is a win.

(For the record, all the comics who finished above me gave up within a year, so haha.)

I drove home with my head held high – which symbolized the pride I felt but also helped me to avoid any head-on collisions. I returned to Manchester two days later, and did well at a gig called the Comedy Balloon. It was 4/4 good gigs, and I was starting to really see a future in comedy.

"I'm going to be a star, Dad," I said to my Mum by mistake. I was helping her with the washing-up, rabbiting on about my exploits. "I can really see God's hand in this. If I keep it up, I may not even need to get a proper job – I'll be getting paid to be funny."

Pride, they say, comes before a fall (or an autumn, if you're not American). Well, it already was the autumn and I was full to the brim with pride – which meant a slip-up was well overdue.

My next gig would be at the Cheeky Monkey Comedy Club in Birmingham. Before that, though, there was the small matter of a date with Helen.

***

It had been ages since I'd been on a date, and I was worried in case the protocol had changed. Feeling desperate, I rang Steve for advice. He told me that the way to impress a girl is to involve her in an activity that you're highly talented at, and thus wow her with your skills. The thing is, I'd tried that before with a previous girlfriend and learned that five hours on Championship Manager doesn't scream "future husband" – particularly if, after you lose 1–0 at home to Bolton, you swear, cry, then blame it on her. Sorry, Catherine.

I realized that I genuinely didn't know how to "do" dating. I'd been single for some time, and before that I'd been in a four-year relationship with a girl called Jess, so it wasn't as though I had a huge frame of reference to draw on. Obviously, with dating, there are the easy, default options of going for a coffee or a beer, but that requires no imagination whatsoever. It's important, surely, to be unique because, unless you are dyscalculic, you only get one chance at a first date.

I worked out, to my horror, that my last official "first date" was back in 1999, but that wasn't a massive help because Quasar was more popular back then, while taking a girl there now would seem pretty creepy. Besides, I don't think a competitive sport like Quasar is a good idea for a first date – particularly if, after she beats you, you swear, cry, then hit her in the face with a laser gun.

As it turned out, all my fretting was pointless. Helen rang me a few hours before I was due to pick her up, to ask whether she might bring a friend along.

"I'm not going to molest you," I said, arguably too impulsively.

"I didn't think you were, Andy," she responded, arguably too nervously. "It's just that my flatmate Sue has been having a difficult time recently, and I don't like the idea of her sitting alone at home all evening. Would it be OK if she came along? Maybe you could bring a friend, too? We could make it a double date!"

"OK, that sounds fun," I answered, with a massive lie.

"Great, where do you fancy going?"

I panicked and went on impulse: "Quasar?"

"I don't think the local Quasar is open any more. Didn't they shut it down when that girl lost four teeth in a laser-rage incident?"

"..........."

"Andy?"

"... So where would you like to go?"

"Well, something like the cinema is fine for me. I hate these guys who try to do something unique and 'out there' on a first date – it's really desperate and off-putting. See you at 7?"

Three hours later I found myself sitting in silence through one of the worst films of all time (I can't remember the name of the film, but it had period costumes, chivalry and Colin Firth in it).

My attempts to chat flirtatiously with Helen were kiboshed by the excruciating sound of sonnets being recited on-screen, and, worse, by the even more excruciating sound of Steve and Sue kissing! How this had happened when it was supposed to be my date was beyond me – particularly given the unhealthy state they were both in.

Steve – a short, well-built Northern Irish man with a mass of dark, tousled hair – had turned up both mysteriously and hideously drunk, unshaven and wearing Bermuda shorts from the nineties.

"You could have put in more effort, Steve," I chastised him.

"I'm just trying to make you look good by comparison. This is the best I could do – good luck."

While Steve's uncanny attempt to act like the Pogues was cringe-worthy, Sue, bless her, as a result of whatever issues she was having, was taking social awkwardness to a new level. Within ten minutes of her arrival, she had twice broken down in tears and run to the toilet (neither time, remarkably, because of Steve's shorts). And yet, somewhere between her frail insecurity and his cretinous drunken bravado, they found each other. Sitting side by side in the packed auditorium, Steve slurred sweet nothings into Sue's ear, reassuring her that everything would be all right and that she was his best friend. If I thought it couldn't get any worse, before even the previews had finished, they were clamped to each other's faces and sounding like a toffee-eating contest in an old people's home. Helen and I just sat there, feeling awkward, for the rest of the film

– my fingers clawing deeper and deeper into the arm-rest and my jaw locking ever tighter. My inner monologue was threatening to riot:

What was she thinking, bringing a friend on a date?! What's next – are we going to end up drinking cider on a street corner while we wait for her Dad to come and pick her up? What was I thinking, bringing Steve?! How did he get so drunk?! Why do women find Colin Firth attractive?!... I wish Quasar was still open.

We will meet my inner monologue again later. He's the voice in my head that speaks when my real voice isn't allowed to. I call him Horatio.

After the film had laboured and shunted to a predictably soppy conclusion, all four of us shuffled out into the lobby, Steve – who, I discovered, had smuggled a hip-flask into the auditorium – holding onto Sue for support. I was about to suggest we go for a drink and a chat, in the hope of redeeming what was, so far, a complete dunghill of an evening. But just as I was forming the word "alcohol" in my throat, the alcohol that had been in Steve's throat, along with a half-digested steak-and-mushroom pie, liberated itself onto the skirt, jumper and eyes of the helpless Sue. Steve reacted as most drunk people do when they vomit, by saying "Whoops" and then giggling, while Sue then made it a hat-trick of tear-induced toilet trips. Helen ran after her, but not before she'd shot me an accusatory look of disgust over her shoulder.

"Should have suggested Championship Manager," I said aloud to nobody in particular. "Come on, Steve, let's get you home."

"I was going to get Sarah's number," he mumbled in protest.

"There's so many reasons why that's not going to happen," I replied, putting his arm over my shoulder and lugging him out of the cinema, as two furious-looking ushers emerged with a mop and bucket. As we left the building, stinking of sick, almost collapsing under Steve's drunkenness and with the sound of crying emanating from the ladies', I may have imagined it, but I'm sure I could hear, somewhere far off, the theme tune from *Some Mothers Do 'Ave 'Em*.

As I drove Steve home, berating him loudly over his strains of "Fairytale in New York", he told me sincerely that he was only tipsy because his brother was over here visiting from Northern Ireland. When I pointed out, accurately, for the second time in a week, that he didn't have a brother, he called me "disrespectful" and tried to exit a moving vehicle.

Oh, and Helen got picked up by her Dad.

***

I rang Helen the next day to apologize for the debacle of the night before. She seemed remarkably unfazed and offered to come to Birmingham with me that night.

"Steve wants to know if Sue would like to see him again," I enquired as we drove down the M6.

"Only if it's on an episode of *Crimewatch*, I would have thought," she replied wryly.

I liked Helen. She was a pretty young lady and had a decent sense of humour, but we'd not spent any proper quality time together until now, and as we got closer to Birmingham, I realized how far apart we actually were.

She had a love of travelling and had just returned from a year-long trip in Vietnam. For me, a good holiday meant Center Parcs, while my only knowledge of Vietnam came from movies starring Chuck Norris.

As you discovered earlier, Helen enjoyed films with Colin Firth. As you discovered in the previous paragraph, I enjoy films with Chuck Norris.

It became evidentially apparent that the only thing we had in common was the fact that the last time we went to the cinema, we'd both had a horrid time. My thoughts turned my Jess, my ex-girlfriend.

She liked Chuck Norris.

I missed her.

"Do you need me to be quiet so you can run over your set?" she asked graciously.

"No, it's fine. I know it."

In my tiny little mind, I was a prodigy – I'd proven that over the space of four gigs. I knew my gags; I knew they would work – simples. And so I didn't spend that afternoon standing in front of my bedroom mirror, with a carrot for a microphone and Subbuteo figures for a crowd, delivering my set over and over and over. I'd done that religiously before all the other nights, and, sure, it had paid dividends. But I didn't need to do that now: I knew what I was doing. (Also, performing to Subbuteo figures makes you feel a bit like you're headlining Lilliput.)

Cheeky Monkey is a gig that still runs in the King's Heath area of Birmingham. Also on the bill that night were Dave Ingram, John Warburton and Junior Simpson. I'd seen Junior in the film, *Love Actually* (he played the DJ) and was nervous and excited to be gigging alongside someone "off of the telly". The gig was in a small back room of a pub, where a large, ungainly black sheet had been draped against one of the walls to act as a backdrop. Add to that the fact that a largely middle-aged crowd had crammed into the restricted space, and it felt less like a comedy night and more like a clandestine meeting of the PTA. This was in the days before the smoking ban, and the intrusive, powerful musk of pipe tobacco lingered in the atmosphere, long after the pipe and its owner had gone home for their tea.

Dave Ingram started the show and compèred well, despite a fairly cold crowd. By the time he introduced John Warburton, they were onside and giggling nicely. "Warby" went on and nailed it, making it look easy, and as the first break arrived I was feeling good and raring to go on and make it five wins from five. Junior reinforced my self-belief:

"They were quiet at the top, weren't they, but they're fine now and up for a good time. You'll have a lovely gig. Have a good 'un."

Dave did five mins at the start of the second half, and by now the crowd were in great voice, heartily chortling at Dave's mix of perky banter and quality material. I was almost giddy with energy and excitement by now, and as I made my way to the stage amid rapturous applause, I even had the audacity to plant a sloppy kiss on Helen's cheek. She was sitting on the end of one of the rows, and wasn't expecting my precipitate act of romance. She smiled coyly and I winked cheekily at her over my shoulder.

"Every weekend, my Dad dresses as a clown for children's birthday parties. It would be more acceptable if anyone had asked him to."

Nothing.

Not a ripple. Not even a smile. They just stared.

It's OK, keep calm, they just need to warm to you. Stay confident…

"A friend of mine asked me if it was difficult to write stand-up. I said you just have to remember the hyphen!"

Niente.

Stay focused…

"I've had a number of girlfriends over the last year. That number is zero…"

Nada.

What was happening? At the Frog, the initial silence had been broken with laughter after a few moments. Here it just seemed to get sucked into a deeper level of silence – the kind of sound vacuum that is usually reserved for coffin-bearing.

Now I was panicking. I could feel beads of sweat grouping on my forehead like excited kids queuing at the top of a waterslide. My face was reddening and I suddenly wanted to be anywhere but there.

Without warning or permission, my mind went completely blank. Presumably Horatio (my inner monologue) had seen the approaching iceberg, realized all hope was lost and decided to jump ship. In my flustered state I was unable to coax him back onto a rapidly sinking vessel, and without his help I plunged to new depths of hopelessness. It's amazing how paralysed you feel in moments of panic. Incapable of recalling any of my material, I just started pulling other people's jokes out of thin air…

"If you stretched a man's veins and arteries out into one long line… he'd be dead."

That joke belongs to a wonderful comedian called Anthony J. Brown, and in his hands it takes the roof off; in my clammy butterfingers, it fell just as flat as my own dire attempts.

This is probably the part of the book that you were waiting for, and I'm only sorry that it's taken 40 pages to get there. It's the one question that all muggles want to ask comedians, and the one question that we all wish we couldn't answer: what's it like to properly, utterly die a death on stage? How does it make you feel?

The fact is that we can all answer that question with astonishing clarity, because we've all been there. Whichever comedian you care to think of has been through that career-threatening rite of passage. And it stays there on the mantelpiece of a comedian's mind. Next to "first laugh" and "first encore" is "first death". It's not that you want it on the mantelpiece, of course – you simply cannot remove it. It stays there always, as a perverse medal of honour.

So, what does it feel like? Different comics will use different analogies: "like sitting on the toilet in front of 500 people"; "like failing all your GCSEs simultaneously"; "like being caught with your secretary in the broom cupboard at work".

All of that rings true, I suppose, but that doesn't really get to the heart of it for me. In my case, it was more like a voice in my psyche – a gentle, calm, heartless voice – saying, "You know that thing that you have always loved, always wanted to do, always hoped you'd be good at, dreamed of, fantasized about? You know that thing you rested your hopes on – the one thing you thought you were best at? Well, you can't do it. You're bad at it. Everyone agrees. Your hopes and dreams have come to nothing."

Having very quickly run out of ideas, but with half of my ten-minute set still remaining, I said something to the crowd that I still can't quite believe:

"I can do impressions."

My desperation had finally broken through to the surface and, impulsively, the whole crowd burst out laughing. They laughed even harder when they subsequently realized what I'd known long before I said I could do impressions: I can't do impressions.

I still don't know why I said it. I've never been able to do accents. My Scottish, Irish and Pirate are all the same voice, while my attempt at Welsh tends to offend any passing Hindus. I think I just said it because I literally couldn't think of anything else to say.

One cringe-worthy attempt at Frank Bruno later, I brought my ill-fated set to an abrupt end.

"This has gone really badly," I confessed. Then, with shoulders hunched and eyes focused on the carpet, I made my way back through the crowd and the tobacco smoke, towards the comics' area. Picking up my bag and shrugging off Warby's attempts at consolation, I wasted no time in making my way through the exit, back onto the High Street and back to the car.

My mind was completely numb, only dully aware of the steady stream of tears making its way down my cheeks. As the Aston Expressway merged with the M6 north, two thoughts struck me.

First: I could never set foot in a comedy club again – the dream was already over.

Second: I'd left Helen behind.

This had all been a horrible mistake.

November

MESSAGE EMPTY

December

I had three gigs penned in for November, all of which I cancelled. In my diary, I Tippexed out the details for the separate nights, then scrawled a different swear-word over the top of each.

Helen and I had decided to go our separate ways. I just had to accept that we were like ships passing in the night… that collided, ran aground and whose crews were brutally tortured by ravenous natives.

Christmas was coming, the time of year when I usually feel so positive. But even the advent of Advent failed to raise my spirits too much on this occasion. Everything was going wrong. For a start, I was single again – single at Christmas: the worst type of single. The offer of a "welcome back discount" from match.com failed to inspire much festive cheer.

Stone-stinking broke, I got a part-time job working in a chocolate factory, packing bars of fudge into boxes. Owing to a large influx of homophobic abuse, however, I quit after four days.

More crucially, though, I felt so devoid of hope at ever finding a career that would satisfy and fulfil me. (You know when you're so depressed that your centre of gravity seems to plummet?) I still desperately wanted to be a professional comedian, but just the thought of going on stage again brought me out in a cold sweat. I even experienced regular night terrors, where the Cheeky Monkey gig would be replayed in my subconscious, but in that weird dreamlike way where the emotions are intensified and everyone has the head of an Alsatian.

Where was God in this? If He wanted me to do this job, how could He allow this to happen? He knew how much I craved being a comedian. He knew that I couldn't bear to fail at the thing I loved most. He knew Mum and Dad would encourage me to get a proper job if there were no signs of progress.

He knew all of that. So what was going on? What had happened to the powerful anointing that had seemed so strong a few short weeks before, but now felt weaker than... this metaphor?

Seriously, where was God?

Was it all bull?

I moped about the house for a month with a permanent feeling of nausea. I had invested so much emotion in this quest. I felt burnt out, dry and empty. It was like having jetlag, although at least jetlag tends to suggest that you have reached your intended destination. My flight had nose-dived shortly after take-off, leaving no survivors.

Or maybe one?

Out of the blue, a lady I'd met socially a few months previously rang me up, inviting me to perform at a Christmas fundraiser she was organizing. When I'd met her initially, it was post-Bath and pre-Birmingham and I was entirely too cocky. I'd told her how I was a comedian (which was debatable and would have left me with an elephantine burden of proof), and she'd mentioned the idea of booking me for a gig. I'd forgotten about it until now, when she told me over the phone about this event to raise funds for her trip to Africa.

"I'm sorry, but I already have plans on that day," I claimed. It wasn't strictly false – a *Thundercats* marathon needs to be planned in advance, I find.

Disappointed, she rang off... only to ring back nine minutes and twenty-seven seconds later.

"So sorry – I got the date wrong. It's actually a week later. Are you free then? I think it's great that you're doing what you've always loved, and we'd love to use your passion for comedy at our event."

45

A flock of butterflies swarmed into my tummy and started flitting around chaotically. She was right, damn it! I'd spent several weeks in a self-perpetuating stupor of lethargy and angst, but what had actually happened? I'd had one bad gig. OK, it was a really bad gig, but I was still 4–1 up in the series. The other gigs hadn't been eradicated by that one torturous experience.

I allege that if that young woman hadn't got her dates befuddled and rung back with such doggedness, I would never have attempted comedy again. My back was already half-turned.

But there was something about the persistence of this lady, the coincidence and timing of the call, and the pull of my heart-strings that it engendered. All of it hinted at something higher, something beyond my immediate control.

The lady on the phone was and is called Tracey Taylor, and I thank God for her to this day.

"I'll do it!" I said. And, having verified that the funds from the Africa fundraiser would go towards building a hospital and not smuggling firearms, we booked it in.

And somewhere in my psyche, where the wreck of an aeroplane lay smashed and smoking, a muffled voice inside the craft shouted, "I'm alive!"

***

The gig itself was largely terrible. It was held in a YMCA sports hall, with about fifty people in attendance – most of whom looked like they'd heard about the concept of laughter, but had never really experienced it first-hand.

The hall itself stank as though sweat-fighters met there twice a week, while the stage was formed from a collection of rotting pallets – one of which snapped whilst the band was playing, lacerating the bassist's Achilles tendon. The stage lighting – I promise you – was provided, not by professional spotlights, but by an industrial-strength torch hanging from the ceiling. The organizational side was so bad, in fact, I could have invited along the team behind the Millennium Dome, and they would have sat there smugly, feeling competent by comparison.

On the front of the glossy programme, the event had been publicized as a "Variety Evening", and, sure enough, the bill was crammed full of different artistes – each with a different lack of skill; each there because Tracey Taylor had called in a favour. Before I went on, the compère introduced a band whose sound can best be described as a cross between Grunge and "Why are my ears bleeding?" Then I went on and did about twenty minutes of awful material which nobody laughed at – partly because their ears were bleeding. Here's an example of the gold I dished out:

"Whenever I go hiking, I always take my Gran with me. Yeah, because her legs are so veiny and weathered, they look like an Ordnance Survey map." (Arguably drawing the deepest silence of the night – and appropriately so.)

I got a similar level of response to the gig in King's Heath; that is, nothing, niente, nada. But somehow it didn't matter. It was no longer a new experience to do badly on stage, and it wasn't going to throw me as it did in Birmingham. I'd already died once, and had come back for more. This audience had no weapons that could hurt me. By the end of the gig, I was actually starting to take a perverse enjoyment from dying on my backside. I found a peace in the deafening silence. Being on stage, telling jokes, felt right. I even managed to smile politely when a woman approached me at the end to say she thought my comedy was about as funny as Third World debt. Steve, who had accompanied me as penance for Vomit-gate, found this hilarious and decided to join in.

"The thing is, though, there's always a chance that Third World debt will get wiped out."

I made a mental note to release a live tiger into Steve's house at the earliest opportunity.

Small consolation was to be found in the fact that the compère for the evening did even worse than me, and was a man for whom the criticism of being "as funny as Third World debt" would have required a massive step-up in ability. At least I was using my own material, so there was a quiet dignity in my defeat. This guy, on the other hand, was telling jokes that could trace their lineage back to Agincourt:

"My Dad and I went on a walking tour of all the B-roads in Norfolk. It was rubbish. Turns out, we should have been on the Norfolk Broads."

That was his highlight. He also emitted a grating laugh after each "punch line" which made me want to cry and be sick simultaneously.

This bloke is the worst comic I've ever seen. He's making me look like a genius.

"Ladies and Gents, thanks for listening. My name's Tony Vino – I'll see you again!"

I hope not.

So that was it – I was back on the wagon. It seems incongruous, perhaps, that tanking could help me rediscover my sense of purpose and drive. But they say that what doesn't kill you makes you stronger (this doesn't apply to beefburgers, cushions or malaria, amongst other things).

You may have been expecting me, having felt the guidance of some higher power drawing me back to comedy, to have nailed that gig. Were you? That, certainly, would be the Hollywood version. "If God wanted you to do that gig, shouldn't you have done really well, rather than stinking the place out?" I've been asked more than once.

Maybe. But this isn't a fairy story or a Hollywood blockbuster. It's just real life.

There's a cult of "rationality" in our culture. We pay lip-service to the idea of basing our lives only on what is provable and testable. But none of us do really. The things that truly matter in life – love, hope, beauty – have no bearing on rationality, and anyone who has ever tried to eke out a living from the Arts knows this.

If I'd followed my head after the shambles that was Stoke YMCA, then my revival would have been short-lived. I would just have thought, "Well, I gave it another go and I'm still useless – and I'm very unlikely to carve a career out of it, so I should just let it die." But life would be so turgid and bland if we genuinely assigned cool logic to all of our decisions. The most memorable and exhilarating moments in life, I believe, are those instances when heart overrules head; when truth supersedes facts.

Nobody goes into comedy because it makes sense: they go into it because it fills their senses.

That gig, in that dusty, smelly venue in parochial North Staffordshire was, I think, God's way of calling me, not to fame or glamour or success, but simply to rely on Him. It was also His way of introducing me to Tony Vino: a man I would meet again despite my hopes to the contrary; a man whose life would, over the ensuing months, start to subtly interweave itself with mine; a man who has grown into a very fine comic and a splendid compère. And the man who is the closest thing I've ever had to a brother.

As I returned to my car, it started snowing. Looking up into the pale, grey sky, I suddenly felt all festive. I'd broken through the fear barrier and I was ready to meet the circuit – and everything it had to throw at me – head on. I felt exhilarated at the prospect of a second foray into comedy, and equally exhilarated at being able to use the word "foray" effectively.

It was beginning to look a lot like Christmas.

***

Feeling slightly embarrassed about my precipitous about-turn, I picked up the phone to the promoters behind the gigs I'd cancelled in November, and told them I'd had a change of heart and was "back on the circuit". My moving story was met with a mixture of disinterest and not-botheredness,[4] but a couple of them happened to have spots available for December, and so for the second time I scribbled details of venues, arrival times and contact numbers into my confused diary. I also Tippexed out the swear-words that I'd scrawled over the Tippexed-out November gigs. It felt like a momentous, defining moment – but that may have had more to do with a regular exposure to noxious corrective fluid than with any real drama.

The first of these gigs was down at a country inn in Wisbech, Cambridgeshire. It was for Mirth Control (the people who offered me the Bath gig) and it constituted a seven-hour round trip for ten minutes of stage-time and no fee. It was a lovely gig and I didn't even feel aggrieved at the colossal journey. In fact, I remember it feeling like I was "touring" – albeit minus any of the trappings of an "actual" touring comedian, such as fans or money.

The landlord of the venue seemed scandalized on my behalf that I'd journeyed so far for so little. "Hey, that's the job," I cockily asserted with a flagrant misuse of the word "job". I'm fairly sure he saw through my arrogant facade when, on offering me £20 petrol money from his own pocket, I leapt at it shouting "My precious!"

I had decided – wisely, I posit – never to use the "Gran's legs look like Ordnance Survey maps" bit again. I replaced it with a new bit I'd written on the way down about *Ready Steady Cook*:

---

4   Not a real word.

I have two issues with this programme. Firstly, nobody ever stays within budget! Ainsley's there, shaking himself around:

"Right, you had £5 – how much did you spend?" [At this point, I did a calypso-style wiggle.]

"£151."

"Oooooh, just over!" [Wiggle.] "Looks like you overdid it with the Unicorn fillets."

Secondly, it doesn't matter what the contestants bring, because half the ingredients are already there anyway!

"Right, what have you got for us, then?" [Wiggle.]

"Cheese. Four types of cheese."

"Oooooh, a mixed bag!" [Wiggle.] "I'm thinking chilli con carne." [Massive wiggle.]

Long journeys are a great setting for running through ideas, and I'm glad I had the courage to throw this "new bit" into the mix, because the crowd loved it. It also attracted passing compliments from the professional acts on the bill: Roger Monkhouse, Tom Wrigglesworth and, once again, Dave Ingram.

My set, which hitherto had been a series of one-liners and puns, ranging in quality from "gently amusing" to "Please God, make him stop!", now had something more substantial. Yes, OK, daytime TV is hardly uncharted territory for the jobbing stand-up, but what it does do is register with the audience and underlie that common ground on which every laugh is built. Thanks to Ainsley, I'd found my "closer" – that bit of material which sticks out from your set as getting the most laughs, and which you therefore finish each set with to leave the audience on a high.

"Well, that went much better than Cheeky Monkey, didn't it?" Dave chuckled. "Glad to see you didn't throw in the towel. At the end of the day, you're always gonna have bad gigs as an open-spot – you just have to bounce back stronger."

Dave had obviously accrued his mentoring techniques from

watching nothing but *Match of the Day*, but I appreciated the sentiment.

As a young sapling in the comedy orchard, it's the little drops of encouragement like this that keep you alive through the spring of your career – a season rich in tumultuous ups and downs. Having a professional comedian say something like "That was good" or "Nice one" engenders disproportionate amounts of happiness and makes you feel like a mighty oak. It would be like Andrea Bocelli saying he liked your voice, or Gordon Ramsey telling you he found your language offensive. It's all very well having Joe Public compliment what you do, but when the specialists approve, the residual glow lasts for days. Ironically, the best description of a fledgling comedian can be attained by paraphrasing a passage in *The Return of the Prodigal Son* by Henri Nouwen:

> A little criticism makes us angry, and a little rejection makes us depressed. A little praise raises our spirits, and a little success excites us. It takes very little to raise us up or thrust us down. Often we are like small boats on the ocean, completely at the mercy of its waves.

A few days after that, I returned to the Comedy Balloon and had another good gig. "The Balloon" is Manchester's longest-running open-mic night. It has been held in a handful of venues over the years, but wherever it's set up camp, it has always provided a really accessible platform for comics new and old to come and hone their craft. It is run by Neil "Spider" Smith, who is one of the real stalwarts of the Manchester comedy scene and a genuine unsung hero.

"It was better than last time," Spider offered after my set, "and that's what you want at this stage. Just keep getting better."

I'd closed with the *Ready, Steady Cook* stuff and it went down a storm. One girl in the front row even spat out her drink. Victor Smithers was also there that night, and it was great to see him again – although he was less forthcoming with fatherly advice than he had been. He wasn't on the bill for the gig, but he'd just turned up because he lived nearby and loved watching comedy. I was gigging in Manchester the next night, too, and Victor very kindly offered me the chance to sleep at his place.

"There's some mild cooking and cleaning involved, but it's a roof over your head and I promise not to strike you," he announced as we walked along Oxford Road together.

I'd been reading some negative stuff about Victor on the online comedy forums. Other comics were logging on to say they found him arrogant and abrasive. When I'd met him at the Frog and Bucket back in October, he had done little to dispel those rumours. But as we strolled through the Manchester night together, I got to see beneath the comedic facade. Yes, he was brash, crude and offensive, but not in isolation. In fact, the farther we got from the Balloon, the more the mask slipped, to reveal a warm underdog of a man.

He had, it transpired, been a fairly successful lawyer over the past few years, but had started to find it vapid and soulless.

"Sometimes I'd turn up at the office at 6 a.m. and think, 'What am I doing here?'"

At the age of thirty, he had decided that if he didn't at least have a go at stand-up, he'd regret it forever.

"I just love making people laugh," he confided. It all sounded very familiar, and rather comforting. We spent hours talking about comedy, girls, football, comedy and girls. I felt like I'd made my first proper comedy friend.

"I like you, Andrew," Victor informed me as the conversation wrapped up. "I don't like your set – I think it's a bit pedestrian, to be fair – but you're a nice guy."

With friends like this…

***

My fourth gig "back on the wagon", then, was at a pub called The Raging Lion in Withington. Victor, as it turned out, was also down to do it – as were a couple of people I'd met at the Frog: Sam Avery and Mike Newall.

This is one of the lovely things about being an open-spot comedian. You see the same folks gig after gig and it allows you to build up a rapport with other newbies – all of you fresh-faced, all starting out, all hopeful that you might one day perform on the same edition of *Live at the Apollo* together.

Once you begin progressing to "twenty-minute" sets and start getting paid gigs all over the country, you can very easily lose touch with the localized hub of young hopefuls you set out with. Of course, sometimes you can't wait to get away from some of the acts who frequent the local pub circuit – as we are about to see.

From experience, I can confidently assert that a comedy night requires a number of things in order to succeed. The main 4 are:
(1) comedians
(2) an audience
(3) a microphone
(4) for bare-knuckle fighting not to break out between (1) and (2).

If you're running a comedy night and you nail those 4, you're probably well on the way. If you fail on (2), (3) and (4), you might like to consider rethinking the night – or possibly a trip to Beachy Head.

The Raging Lion is a lovely pub between Withington and Didsbury (and about two miles away from where I now live). The staff are polite, the beer is good and aesthetically, I would say it's one of my favourite pubs in Manchester. However, none of that makes it a shoe-in for a comedy night.

The promoter – if you can call him that – was one of those people who you meet from time to time in comedy who think that putting a microphone in the middle of a pub and getting people to talk into it transforms you into some kind of industry professional. If I remember rightly, he was some kind of failing actor who thought that staging and hosting his own comedy night would add to his "range". It certainly added to the wide range of people who thought he should have been shot on sight.

I confess I don't actually remember his name – in the same way that it's possible to block out painful childhood memories. Let's call him Phil.

In all seriousness, if you surveyed the entire comedy fraternity and asked them what the major prerequisite for a successful comedy night is, I am 80 per cent sure that about 75 per cent would assert the same thing: a captive audience. (It would have to be a late-afternoon survey, to ensure we were all up and about.)

Comedy is not like music. If comedy and music were siblings, music would be the younger, more docile child who would happily play in the corner and keep out of trouble. Comedy, on the other hand, would be the older, spoilt brat of a kid who refused to let his younger brother or sister take any of the limelight and couldn't bear to be anything other than the centre of attention.

There's a reason why, when you go to a pub or coffee house, they don't play recordings of Paddy McGuiness through the speakers. Actually there are two reasons, but the less contentious one is that the human brain cannot take in more than one train of thought at a time. Gentle music can meld with, enhance and complement a lovely latte-based chat, but speech on top of speech just clashes.

How does this relate to a comedy night? Well, it's quite simple. People who go to the pub for a drink and a chat, only to find themselves surrounded by a comedy night that they have paid nothing to be a part of, don't listen; in fact, they do what they came to do – have a drink and a chat. But when you're on stage trying to talk yourself, and there are people trying to listen to you with a view to laughing, having another stream of speech impinge on that just ruins it – I mean completely ruins it, like throwing a balloon into the goal-mouth during a penalty shoot-out.

You can dip in and out of a song without it losing its effect. You may miss some of the lyrics, granted, but you can subconsciously absorb the chords, the tune, the tone etc. You cannot subconsciously absorb a joke. Comedy needs a captive audience because comedy is needy and selfish. An audience made up of people who aren't there for "the funny" won't laugh anywhere near as much as an audience who have invested in the gig. It doesn't have to be a financial investment, you understand; there are stacks of free comedy nights which are a delight to play. It's the emotional investment that is key for comedy.

It's the reason why "corporate gigs" are almost always a nightmare, and the reason why my Mum will often look over the top of her *Gardener's World* magazine during *Mock the Week* and say, "This isn't very funny, is it?"

Watching comedy requires as much focus as performing it does, which is why when a night goes well, the audience really feels like a part of something special.

So, here we have the primary problem of the night in question. The gig was held in the main body of the pub and there was no ticketing system, so people could – and did – just wander in and out, chatting and heckling as they went.

"It'll be good experience for you," chimed failed-actor-Phil, as he clocked me cringing at the steady thoroughfare of people strolling across the stage area to get to the toilet. (For "stage area" read "dusty rug from the 1950s").

"I know from my work as an actor that it's nourishing to play in challenging environments."

"Yeah, you're right," I said somewhat naively. Had he said

that to me more recently, I might have done something horrible to him – like setting fire to his shoes or getting him front-row Paddy McGuiness seats.

I rejoined Victor in a corner of the pub. He was chatting to a sketch troupe called Stupid, Stupid and Stupid, who were also fairly new to the scene. I immersed myself in the patter and we all joked and laughed about the absence of any ticketing and the state of the performing area – although the laughter was the most prodigious exaggeration of reality since Dick Van Dyke told Walt Disney Studios he could do a convincing Cockney accent.

Then fate seemed to take a turn for the better. Smithers was part-way through his seemingly trademark "I'm off for a poo now – you're free to come but it will mean the end of our friendship..." when a small but perfectly formed group of student nurses glided into the room. Victor spat out his water and gurned.

"Cashback!" exclaimed Stupid.

"Ding dong!" followed up Stupid.

"Back of the net!" cried Stupid. The three of them laughed at their own lechery, whooping and hi-fiving. Wanting to join in with the vacuous bravado, I pitched in:

"Whoopsie Daisy!"

No one laughed and they all walked off to chat to the girls. I stood on my own, trying to work out the last time I'd used the phrase "Whoopsie Daisy!" in public, and why I'd felt the need to wheel it out on this occasion.

"See you in a bit, Andy – I'm off to chat to my future wives," Victor confided, Mormonly. Presumably, emptying his bowels had been moved down the list of things to do, and was now behind "Scare and offend pretty ladies."

I've never been good at "chatting up" girls. I can chat to them, and I can ask them out, but "chatting up" – the idea of feeding women your best lines – has always seemed so superficial and forced. If I want to impress a woman, I'll ask her to test me on late 80s/early 90s football trivia.

People seem to think that comedians must be really good at chatting up girls, because we're all so frightfully quick-witted. But that's unadulterated nonsense: no comedian likes performing to an audience of one. For me, trying to chat up a girl one to one just feels like performing at a poorly promoted gig – a gig which, to boot, I'm unlikely to get rebooked for.

You might also be under the impression that saying you're a comedian would convey an enigmatic sexiness to a lady, but that's equally bunkum. Most of the time they simply don't believe you, and, worse, if they do, they say the first thing which springs into their mind, which is invariably "Ooh, tell us a joke!"

Comedy is the only profession where you are asked to prove what you do on the spot. You don't find out someone is a soldier and instantly demand that he shoot you in the face.

Anyway, the point is that I can't/don't like to chat up girls, and we all remember what happened the last time I got together with a lady at a comedy night. (Read the last page of "September" if you don't.)

As Stupid, Stupid, Stupid and Desperate returned from their mission with fleas in their ears (arguably from the flea-infested 1950s carpet), I began to notice something I hadn't spotted during the preliminary chat: Stupid was a psychopath.

I hadn't picked up on it until now because Stupid and Stupid had done most of the talking, and they were thoroughly pleasant individuals. But now Stupid came to the fore, cursing and spitting – genuinely angry that these health practitioners seemed immunized against his advances.

"What's the point of doing comedy if you can't get some ****** action?! Who do they think they are, stuck-up *****! ****** nurses thinking they're ****** better than me! Well, they can **** right ***!

Confused as to why he had replaced half his words with little stars, I wandered off to prepare my set-list. "He's a bit over the top," I thought. I certainly didn't think "He'll probably head-butt a man in the front row in about forty minutes." Which is why Derren Brown is on TV, and I'm not.

In reality, you don't see that many brawls on the circuit. I think I've witnessed no more than four over the course of about 600 gigs. But I need to do my parental guidance thing here, so please be aware that the following contains scenes of moderate peril, and should not be read to young children before the watershed.

Failed-actor-Phil compèred the show and was comprehensively woeful. He started by telling the audience that he hadn't written any material and was "almost always garbage anyway" – which is what you want to hear at the start of a comedy night.

I'll talk about what I think makes a good compère in due course, but let's just agree for now that it doesn't involve dashing the audience's faint hopes of having a good evening within the first thirty seconds. Failed-actor-Phil went on to say how he had never seen any of the acts on the bill before, "except Victor Smithers, but he didn't do very well when I saw him", and the crowd would be wrong, therefore, to raise their hopes too high. During this first minute of pure comedy gold, at least four pub-goers strolled right across the stage area, practically pushing past failed-actor-Phil, on their way to the bog.

Before bringing on the first act, Sam Avery, failed-actor-and-dreadful-compère-Phil decided to tell a "funny story" about his trip to the doctor. There was a fleeting moment where it looked like the nine-minute anecdote might be buffered by a punch line, but instead it concluded with the doctor telling failed-actor-and-dreadful-compère-and-hopeless-raconteur-Phil that he had contracted gout.

"It may not be funny, but it is true."

There were other adjectives to define it. The mood in the room can be best summed up simply by looking at Edvard Munch's picture *The Scream*. Failed-promoter-Phil just stood there crestfallen while six or seven punters edged past him to have a tinkle. The Santa hat he was wearing to adorn the night with festivity adorned him, ironically, with the look of a really sad elf.

It was from this melange of increasingly dour compèring and decreasingly interested crowd members that a singular tension arose; a tension that would only be broken by the sound of bone crushing septum.

Sam Avery and Victor battled valiantly against a tide of chatter and apathy in the first section, while I gamely delivered my set with as much confidence as I could muster – stopping once to help manoeuvre a lady in a wheelchair towards the toilet.

Then Phil (the failed everything) announced the next "turn" to the stage: Stupid, Stupid and Stupid.

Sketches don't really work at comedy nights. They certainly don't work when they are invaded by people bound for the loo. They absolutely don't work when one of the artistes (Stupid) breaks off mid-line to head-butt a passing heckler (well, at least that's my opinion).

In fairness to Stupid, it was technically dextrous. The curtailing of his lines to the contact with the nose happened in one swift movement – like a top-class wicket-keeper who catches the ball and dismantles the stumps in a single sweep. Leaping like a salmon or a man shot from a cannon, the front of his skull connected perfectly with the heckler's gulliver, sending both of them crashing to the floor as dust and red, red krovvy mingled together in the smoky air.

Now, let me clarify: I don't think this was a good thing to happen. Yes, the heckler had been shouting things all night at various acts and all of us had our hackles up, but that didn't mean he deserved the flying Glasgow kiss he received as thanks. Violence cannot be condoned in comedy – or anywhere else – and whilst a persistent heckler is annoying, he should be taken down with wit and verbal dexterity, rather than a vicious blow to the face.

Well, it all kicked off after that. The victim's mates – who clearly thrived on a bit of the old ultra-violent – piled in to Stupid, with Stupid and Stupid joining the mix in support of their lunatic friend. There were pint glasses, rubber chickens and other assorted props flying everywhere. Sam Avery, Mike Newall and I vidied what we must do, and tried to break it up, while Victor Smithers went over to protect the student nurses. (He later claimed to have been head-butted in the groin, and could one of them give him a check-up?)

Failed-actor-Phil didn't get involved in the mêlée, and when the ruckus died down he was nowhere to be seen. I found his Santa hat hanging from the rickety mic stand. He never promoted another gig in Manchester.

"Well," I thought, as I left the venue two hours later, having helped to mop up spilt blood and beer and pack away the last of the rubber chickens, "at least nobody's going to remember me using the phrase 'Whoopsie Daisy'. Every cloud…"

***

Christmas had come and the bells were ringing out. The weather outside was slightly less frightful than the number of Snowballs Dad had consumed before midday, while, at the same time, putting the finishing touches to the copious lunch we were all about to enjoy and then, very quickly, regret.

After a month of largely positive come-back gigs, I was feeling much more festive than at the start of the month. The Santa hat I'd taken from The Raging Lion – after failed-elf-Phil had left it in his wake – was seated comfortably on my head, I had a steaming tankard of mulled wine in my hand, a song in my heart, and I was looking forward to watching *Mary Poppins* for the forty-eighth time.

As Dad fried and roasted the final accoutrements to the meal – stopping, every so often, to re-open the advocaat – the rest of us sat around in the lounge, perusing our respective piles of presents and prophetically wearing elasticated waists.

Gifts-wise, it had been a good haul and everybody seemed happy. The remote-controlled socks I'd asked for hadn't been forthcoming, because, apparently, said my sister, there's no such thing. Still, I had an ample selection of books and DVDs to studiously work my way through over the winter break, plus the sealed promise of a colossal post-turkey, belt-undone-and-trousers-unbuttoned-with-mouth-wide-open-and-saliva-dripping-out nap to look forward to. As you can observe, Christmas in the Kind household is always a magical affair.

I didn't actually stop believing in Father Christmas until I was ten years old. The spell was broken when, on searching the house for presents, I uncovered a Santa Claus costume in my Dad's wardrobe. I stopped believing after that. I then looked in my Mum's wardrobe and stopped believing in Catwoman and nurses. (NB: That is a joke. Please do not take it literally or get in touch with Social Services.)

What's truly marvellous about Christmas in our house is that we always get the whole family together – Mum, Dad, Gran, my sister and brother-in-law – eat a lot of trifle, watch a lot of bad TV and play loads of games. We are quite a competitive family, and so each game carries with it an intricate scoring system. The scores for each game are fed into a league table, and at the close of Boxing Day the overall winner gets a prize – which is usually the rest of the trifle.

Risk is my favourite yuletide game to play, although we're all Christians in our household and Risk with Christians is rubbish. Seriously, Risk played solely by Christians is a waste of time – because nobody wants to attack; we just keep sending in missionaries and aid packages. Eventually, we just sign a peace treaty and everybody gets one point each.

While we're on the subject of board games, can I add that I always find the boast on a lot of games a bit weird. If you look on the box of many classic board games, you'll see: "Suitable for ages 8–80!" As though that's something to be proud of! Well, my Gran is 83. What's she supposed to do – sit on her own in the corner while I gallivant around London as a massive shoe? Classic board games, as it transpires, are largely fascist. OK, she's not up for Twister, but aside from that she's fully *compos mentis*. (This is, of course, dependent on the alcohol content of the trifle.)

There's no age limit on Singstar, though, and she flipping loves that – she even beat me on this occasion! Singstar, if you have no inkling as to what I'm going on about, is that karaoke-style game on the PS3. You plug in a couple of microphones and try to sing along to various tunes, and the better your rendition, the more points you get.

Gran and I were tied for first place. Dad would usually be out in front, but a glut of festive cocktails had seen him finish last in every game – except Twister where he narrowly defeated Gran. He would normally triumph at Monopoly, but we were forced to veto playing that this year, because all the money had gone missing – and when I say missing, I mean that Steve and I had "borrowed" it and tried to go to the pub. Massive fail. Instead, Dad now lay snoring on the sofa, still wearing his apron and drooling copiously.

Wil, my brother-in-law, looked to be out in front in the Gamer's Championship after a sterling performance in Scrabble where he somehow managed to get "gonorrhoea" – which got him 100 points and a free check-up.

Anyway, it was deadlock between my Gran and I as the final challenge hove into view. As I mentioned, I'm a hugely competitive individual at times – I'd swim in sewage if there was a league table and a trophy involved. So going head to head with Gran on what is essentially for her unfamiliar territory seemed like a good way of making a push for trifle-flavoured victory. I even chose the song; I thought, there's no way she'll know Dizzee Rascal.

Apparently, however, she really relates to Dizzee and thinks his lyrics perfectly capture the urban *zeitgeist*. She battered me and took the title – and with it, the trifle.

Full of anger, regret and turkey, I settled down to watch *Lord of the Rings*. It had got to the bit where you start wondering how close Sam and Frodo actually are, and why nobody ever goes to the toilet (after all, Gandalf's not a young wizard), when my phone rang, taking me by surprise and jerking Dad momentarily from his stupor.

"Hiya, Andy. It's Wayne from Ribbed Comedy."

"Hi, mate. Happy Christmas!"

"Yeah, yeah, anyway look, I'm booking for a new gig in Crewe starting in January."

"Right?"

"Well, I promised to get you back in at Fat Cats, so thought I'd offer you a spot. It's on the 23rd of January. Any good?"

"Well, I haven't got my diary to hand at the moment, mate, and to be honest, Christmas Day isn't the most conveni—'

"It's £20."

"What time do you want me there?"

I don't know whether Wayne did it on purpose – I presume he did. Nobody makes a work call on Christmas Day if they can avoid it. If he did mean it – and I've never thought to ask him – then he is nothing short of a genius.

In one sense, it was a bit of an affront to interrupt the precious time I was spending with my family. In another, balloon-poppingly awesome sense, Wayne was offering me a present that you couldn't buy in the shops; a gift that not even Father Christmas could fit in his sledge. He was offering me money to perform comedy.

"Merry Christmas," he said as he rang off.

It was. I had my first paid gig.

January

January is the weirdest of all months, with all of us torn by conflicting emotions. On the one hand, there is the mourning of the festive season. You've overdosed on stuffing and Morecambe and Wise; you're having to go cold-turkey; you're craving hot turkey. Your bank account is barren, while fresh debts sprout up everywhere.

On the other hand, there is that overwhelming, all-encompassing sense of hope. This is a new year, a chance to plant new seeds of purpose that can blossom and flourish, while at the same time weeding out the negatives from the previous twelve months. One thing I try to weed out early at the start of a new year is any extraneous gardening metaphor.

Andy Kind was a quarter of the way through his first year in comedy, and had decided to start the year as he meant to go on – by referring to himself in the third person. However, he soon realized that this attempt would create difficult continuity issues, and so gave up after one paragraph.

I was feeling good about life, and about comedy. The sub-arctic conditions were making one's daily ablutions more ponderous (during the summer months, you forget just how cold a toilet seat can be in January). However, despite the freezing conditions, my comedy hopes had been reheated. Even though I'd only been performing for a few short months, and in that time had only managed a smattering of gigs, I felt a certain sense of achievement merely for sticking in there – a bit like in *Gladiators*, where a contestant playing Duel might somehow manage to hang on for the full thirty seconds without getting toppled, despite a barrage of blows.

A lot of people attempt stand-up comedy. Most people only ever attempt it once. To get on stage a second time is usually a good sign; to make it past ten gigs usually ensures you'll make it to twenty, and so on. I'd done nine gigs, and only one of those had felt like a complete disaster. I'd also had some cracking advice along the way, especially from a chap named Gary Delaney, who is regarded by many new acts as the Yoda of the comedy world. (He also happens to be one of the best joke writers in the world – even better than Yoda, who, to be fair, lets himself down by putting the punch line at the start of the sentence.) Gary had told me: "Having a bad gig isn't the mark of failure, but getting back on stage after a bad gig *is* a sign of success." Then he vanished in a puff of smoke.

So I felt good. I felt even better when I did the first "Beat the Frog" of the New Year and won the competition, beating Victor in the clap-off. And with the Holy Grail that is a paid gig on the horizon, I was a-flutter with hope and excitement that the maverick gamble I'd taken back in September might actually pay off.

Then I talked to my Dad.

***

At that time, my Dad was working down in London four days a week, and so sometimes, to save Mum trouble and accrue easy brownie points, I'd take Dad to Stoke Station on a Monday morning.

As I chauffeured him the four miles or so on what was a typically dreary January morning, we were enjoying a reasonably jovial and affable chat, reminiscing about New Year's resolutions from time immemorial and debating the issue of Gran's Dizzee Rascal obsession. Then, quite suddenly and without prior consultation, he said, "Have you found yourself another job yet?"

This, naturally, was a rhetorical question; if I had found a job, I wouldn't have been permanently wearing a tracksuit, and he knew that. I quipped that they don't display job vacancies on UK Gold or CBeebies. Was I really expecting a laugh from that?

He then proceeded to insinuate that I was a wastrel. I'm not entirely sure what that means, but I think it's one of those phrases that you can only use if you're a parent or a teacher. (The same rule applies to the phrases "I'll have your guts for garters" and "Woe betide you".)

In essence, I think what Dad was saying – though I can't be sure, because for most of the journey I was replaying scenes from the movie *Weekend at Bernie's* in my mind – was that I couldn't just lazily amble through life and expect to do whatever I felt like doing; life was more serious than that. Now, naturally I had that same nagging conviction in my own mind, and I didn't really need him to spell it out for me. Ironically, as we reached the station, he presented me with a letter in which he had done just that.

"Don't waste your potential, son. See you on Thursday."

"........."

And so let's take a look at my route into comedy from a different perspective; that is, the perspective of the people who taught me to laugh.

I love my Dad. Obviously, I don't tell him this, because I'm English and not gay – and therefore, emotionally stunted.

I'm not sure where this very Anglo-Saxon malaise comes from – the inability of fathers and sons to talk openly about feelings. Presumably, we're banned from showing any genuine affection to one another in case the Nazis sense weakness and try to take Dover.

But affection and admiration there is, nonetheless – not least because my Dad has qualities that I only wish I, myself, possessed. He is a hugely intelligent and practically dextrous man, who has never been one for showmanship and has always kept himself to himself. The many gifts he does possess are kept shrouded in a thick veil of modesty. In essence, he's me in negative.

Dad's challenge to me outside of Stoke Station wasn't born out of intolerance or passivity, but genuine concern. It must have been mind-boggling for both my parents to have me take such a wild detour in life. I mean, how many people do you know who go into comedy? It's hardly a standard graduate job, is it?

My career prospects must have seemed rock-solid from Mum and Dad's perspective. I was Head Boy at both primary and secondary school; I excelled at both GCSEs and A-Levels; I then attended one of the top ten Universities in the country to study Modern Languages, and got a very fine Second Class Honours degree. They had done a grand job bringing me up, and were perhaps waiting expectantly to see which of the *Guardian* Top 100 graduate programmes I would glide sleekly into. And then I did... nothing.

I came out of University and spent six months sitting down. I don't really know why.

Maybe there was just too much choice? With my academic talent, I had a good chance of landing a decent graduate job. But, there again, maybe there wasn't enough choice? All the graduate jobs on offer looked humdrum and wearisome. So I remained motionless. To onlookers, it must have looked like I was in some kind of half-sleep, but I actually think – without wanting to sound trite and self-indulgent – that I was starting to wake up. Life had suddenly stopped being so linear, and it had jolted me from my torpor.

When you're fourteen, you decide which GCSEs you want to take from the limited options available. You get told that you can't just do PE, and that you have to do a language, regardless of whether you ever plan to go to Germany or, if you take Latin, ancient Rome. Two years later, you decide which three or four GCSE subjects you want to specialize in. You get told that you still can't do just PE, but you can at least stop Latin, because of the universal discovery that all anyone can remember anyway is "*Quintus fascus est.*"

Then, at eighteen, you settle on one of your three or four A-Level subjects to "study" at University. You can at this stage just do PE and try to make it sound important by calling it Sports Science. Equally, you can just do the subject which you've found the least hassle and which you think might, further down the line, get you introduced to Audrey Tautou or Thierry Henry. (At least, that's my story.)

Eventually, after three years at University, you enter the real world and finally ask the question, "What do I actually want to do with my life?"

The answer for me had been the same since my mid-teens, but I was never encouraged to put it on a UCAS form.

I found French easy. I breezed through GCSE, A-Level, and even found degree level relatively straightforward. But I didn't love it. I had friends at Uni who were constantly "on fire" for their studies. My flatmate, Jerrard, chose to study the two things he found the most interesting – Computer Programming and Anatomy. (The irony being, of course, that the more he spent talking about computer programming, the less likely it became that he would ever see, up close, anyone's anatomy.)

But to see people with such a burning passion for what they were being taught made me green – I think with envy, but at least twice it was alcohol poisoning.

The recurrent problem had always been that you can't teach my passion. You can't give academic instruction on what I love.

I studied French because I felt it was the correct protocol and I understood the need to have a good degree. But I never wanted to be a French teacher or a translator or blockade a port. From academic success to academic success, there was one thing above all others that I wanted to do; one thing I felt I could do better than anything else; a career path I desperately wanted to pursue in spite of a complete dearth of opportunities: comedian.

So, having left Warwick and spent half a year studiously watching boxed sets, taking various clubs to European glory on Championship Manager and seeing how many Wispas I could eat in an hour, I eventually went to work in telesales. I chose that over the variety of other jobs open to me, including telemarketing, telephone account managing, web account managing, web-advertising, web-sales, new media sales, half-price sales, sails on a ship and Sale near Manchester.

I hated it, and quit.

Poor Mum and Dad. What had happened to their bright, dynamic son? Why was he stalling like this? They would always be proud of me, of course, but they could see their hopes of a high-flying son fading like the memory of Latin grammar.

Had they done something wrong?

Of course, they hadn't. They had done so much right. They had brought me up to have confidence in myself, to believe that I was capable of great things, and to love laughter. Ironically, it was my Dad's *Blackadder* and *Fawlty Towers* videos that lit the fire of ambition within me all those years before. More than that, it's the combination of my Dad's dry wit and my Mum's maniacal energy that forms the basis for my sense of humour, and my act.

Mum and Dad have been largely responsible for my burning desire to spread joy and laughter – because joy and laughter, unambiguously, is what they gave me.

I think my abrupt announcement that I was going to do it as a career took them completely by surprise – plus the fact that the very idea of becoming a professional comedian seemed so alien, so ludicrous, and so financially precarious, that they possibly felt unable to lend it their full vocal support. After all, they hadn't invested so much to have me fritter it away on a boyhood fantasy.

As my Dad got out of the car and lugged his heavy bags into Stoke Station, a strong sensation of guilt grew inside me. I was letting him down.

One thing is certain. By far the greatest ambition for any son is to make his own Dad proud; by far the greatest fear is that he won't. Within this tension, more than anything else, lies the reason why venturing into comedy was, for me, such a risky roll of the dice, but also why it was the one thing I needed to do. If I was ever going to be successful at anything, it was going to be this. If Dad was ever going to see me thrive, it would be through this. If I was ever going to show him the absolute best that I could be, it would be in this. The chances of success were, I conceded inwardly, very small, but I remained stoic in my resolve and certain of my predicament: comedy was all or nothing.

All in an instant, in the light of what my Dad had said, the £20 I'd been offered to perform ten minutes of stand-up in a Cheshire pub ceased to be solely a piece of paper with the Queen's head on. It was the legacy of twenty-five years of parenting.

A £20 note. Quite a flimsy thing on which to pile so much hope.

***

It was a densely foggy evening as I drove across the Staffordshire border towards Crewe. I hate driving through fog. It's not that I'm scared of crashing, you understand – I'm just always slightly concerned I might go back in time.

The gig was at a pub called The Witches' Coven, which in name seemed to promise so much, but ultimately was a massive let-down – a bit like Michael Owen, or London. Having never been there before, I had genuine concerns about turning up as a Christian. It turned out to be just a working pub, rather than an actual centre for witchcraft, but I had feared taking the gig might be the worst decision from a Christian since MC Hammer decided he wasn't a fan of tight-fitting trousers.

The building itself dated from approximately a long time ago[5] and had bits falling off it. The brickwork was hugely in need of repointing, and round the back there was a group of lads using one of the walls to play Jenga. Huddled around outside the entrance were a group of old boys holding tankards of ale.

"Smokers' corner?" I enquired cheerily as I passed them.

"Safer standing outside," came the perfunctory reply.

Wayne the promoter had told me he wouldn't be there for this particular gig, but that I should introduce myself to the landlord on arrival. Walking over to a portly man in a lumberjack's shirt who had his belly balanced on the bar, I noticed that there was a distinct lack of comedy paraphernalia, most notably a microphone, a stage area or an audience.

"Hi, I'm Andy, one of the comedians. Are you Mick?"

"Who's asking?"

"I am. I'm one of the comedians."

"I'm Mick."

"Great. Do you need any help setting up the speakers and mic?"

"We don't have any. Don't you bring your own?"

I learned from Wayne the next day that he'd spoken to Mick and verified that they had all the correct equipment for staging the night's entertainment. Mick was apparently "changing the barrel" at the time and so wasn't really listening. As a result, they were about as prepared for hosting comedy as I would be for giving birth. (That is, not at all – I'm not Arnold Schwarzenegger from *Junior*.)

This is something that happens a lot when pubs try to put on comedy nights: they don't have a clue. You can instruct them as

---

5   I can't be bothered to do the research.

much as you like down the phone, and they'll fob you off and say, "It'll be a good night", and then you turn up to find it's more likely to be "Good night, Vienna."

For the record, unless otherwise stated, comedians do not bring their own equipment. What happens is, we turn up for the gig; everything else should already be there, prepared. In the same way, I don't waltz into Nandos with a chicken under my arm.

Beyond not having any sort of voice-amplification device, Mick, in his wisdom, had failed to promote the gig in any way. It's disturbing and upsetting how many venue owners appear to have that *Field of Dreams* mentality: "If we book it, they will come." Consequently, there were no punters in for the show. On reflection, even if someone had rocked up to enquire speculatively about it, being probed with "Who's asking?" by a burly man in a Brokeback Mountain shirt would have proven sufficient for a night in with a DVD.

The other comics – Dave Twentyman and Danny Deegan – arrived about ten minutes after me, both of them laughing when I said there was no mic, then cursing loudly when they discovered I wasn't joking.

"You'll just have to do it acapulco lads," Mick suggested, malapropismally. "Just shout your material!"

"If I wanted to drive around the country shouting at people in public, I'd become a Christian," jibed Twentyman, caustically. At this juncture, some fellow believers might have pedantically highlighted that his remark, though witty and spontaneous, was nevertheless a gross generalization and could properly only be applied to soapbox evangelists and not the entire body of the church. But that's why people hate us.

"Where's the nearest pub – I'll see if I can borrow something from there," asserted Twentyman, heroically.

"Danny and I will try to drum up support from passers-by," I added.

And so, in a mini version of *Challenge Anneka*, we went off to try to create a comedy night out of nothing.

Within the hour, Dave was back at The Witches' Coven with a karaoke machine that he'd borrowed from an old people's home. Danny and I had managed to charm a dozen or so people into the arena (and when I say "charm", I absolutely mean "plead with tearfully and bribe with Bishop's Finger").

Buoyed and preoccupied by our courageous team effort to flog a dead horse, we had failed to notice one thing – the compère hadn't turned up. Perturbed but unabashed, I rang Wayne to ask who was down to compère.

"It's a guy called Phil. He runs a gig at The Raging Lion in Withington."

"Did he confirm for tonight?"

"No, I booked him back in November…"

"Yeah, that's game over."

I couldn't believe it. Failed-actor-Phil was down to compère! This guy was fast turning into my nemesis (by which I don't mean he was my second-favourite ride at Alton Towers). Obviously, he hadn't turned up because he had vanished from the face of the comedy circuit in the aftermath of Stupidgate, and was possibly to be found somewhere in rural Somerset, living as a goat.

"We're going to have to do the show without a compère," I confessed to Dave and Danny as I rang off.

"Short of an act, lads?" came an ominous voice from behind the bar.

"Er… no?" I squeaked, in the least convincing lie since Henry VIII told Anne Boleyn, "It's not you, it's me."

"I'll warm 'em up for you, boys. I spoke at a rally once."

We didn't have the energy to stop him, nor the resolve to ask what sort of rally it was. So we let Mick compère.

What exactly is a compère? And what, precisely, is their role within a comedy night? There are great swathes of people who don't have the foggiest – including, it would seem, Microsoft Word 2007, which concedes its ignorance by underlining the word "compère" in red every time I type it.

I can tell you straight off the bat what a compère isn't. It isn't someone who goes on before the other comedians, insults as many people as possible, does a few Les Dawson jokes, threatens to take his pants down and show his angry penis if people don't start having a good time, and then says, "Right, well, someone else can have a go now. I don't know his name but he looks like a rat."

And that's the reason allowing Mick to compère was the worst idea since... well, no, actually it was *the* worst idea. Had we screened footage of Vietnamese war atrocities and forced everyone to stare at the screen like *A Clockwork Orange*, then squirted iodine into their eyes while laughing maniacally, it would have seemed charmingly hospitable compèred to Mick (*sic*).

He was under the impression that comedy is all about ripping the hell out of people, and that to be a successful stand-up all you need to do is shout very loudly, pepper every sentence with a liberal number of f's and c's, and then wait for the laughter to roll in.

By the time the first act, Danny Deegan, sloped onto stage, half of the dozen people we'd begged to watch had left, leaving a mere handful of punters – one of whom was a Doberman.

"Thanks for sticking around," Danny told the select group in front of him.

"You promised us a drink, fella," came the reply. "We'll leave when we get it."

Danny rallied valiantly in the face of such apathy, but the damage had already been done by Mick, and the night became impossible to negotiate from a comedic point of view. During the break, after they'd received their bribe in full, the rest of the audience did indeed vacate the premises in a very deliberate, unified way – even the Doberman refused to make eye-contact. It left the night in ruins, all thanks to Mick, and meant that Twentyman and I wouldn't get to perform.

It's a pretty spectacular trick to single-handedly vandalize a comedy night, but credit where it's due – Mick did just that. From having booked the comedy night in the first place, to failing to advertise it in the slightest, and finally to abusing his own punters with the threat of a vengeful willy, Mick had comprehensively covered all the bases. All he would need to do now was refuse to pay the acts who hadn't actually performed, and his inverted Midas-man trick would be complete.

And that's what he did. After all that rigmarole, I never got that £20.

I didn't tell my Dad.

January is always a quiet month for comedy, with punters preferring to recoup Christmas losses rather than continue along on the excess bandwagon. I did another two gigs before the end of the month – another for Mirth Control, in Stroud, and then a gig for a bloke calling himself Spiky Mike in Derby.

They both went well, and the whole Mick saga actually paid dividends, as I condensed the whole episode into a highlights package and recounted it to the near-incredulous crowds. It was the first time I'd actually included any real story-telling in my set (and, moreover, anything that was actually true). Up until then, if I'm honest, I had mainly dealt in the standard fare for new acts – trite jokes about my appearance (how I can sometimes be mistaken for a camper version of Ross Kemp), how rubbish (insert name of home town) was, and how chavs/scallies/kevs/people from Liverpool walk and speak in a silly way. This sort of easy humour forms the backbone of most new acts,[6] and there's nothing wrong with that when, in those early days, you just need laughs to keep

---

6   Most newbies talk about their own appearance, and not how I look strikingly similar to a camp Ross Kemp.

you going. It may be junk food, but it stops you starving to death.

But after a while, you realize that, unless you want to be like any other open-spot, you are going to have to be more personal, more unique. There are few things more disappointing in comedy than watching a professional act churning out hackneyed banalities about how men are different from women, old people smell and the London Underground is annoying. Or, even worse, when acts stick to a tried-and-tested formula of imagining "Person A performing Action B in the style of Person C". ("What if David Cameron addressed the Commons like Robert De Niro from the film *Taxi Driver*?")

(NB: I'm confident that I still use material – probably always will – that fellow professionals see as bland or safe or formulaic, and of course there is a massive tranche of subjectivity to everything I'm saying, so please don't think I consider myself to be some kind of comedy oracle. Hey – this just came to me – wouldn't it be funny if the Oracle from the *Matrix* films was just a Scouse chav?)

Anyway, the point is that it felt nice to be idiosyncratizing my material and beginning to break out of that archetypal open-spot mould. And by the time I knew where I was, it was February.

And I was ready to enter my first official national competition.

February

Before I got into stand-up, I imagined that the life of a comic would ultimately consist of travelling the country in a magic bus, solving mysteries, performing to sell-out theatres in the evening, then hooking up for after-show drinks with Suggs and Les Dennis. I also thought it would instantly make me a babe-magnet. So far, I had massively overestimated – although part of that can be traced to the fact that I still think the phrase "babe-magnet" is acceptable for use in common parlance.

As yet, I wasn't hanging around with any minor celebrities – although my mate Howard has been mistaken for Simon Mayo, and I once brushed past Aled Jones in a corridor. On the ladies front, I had briefly dated Helen, if "dated" is indeed the correct euphemism for "made myself look like a massive twonker in front of..." Aside from that, the harvest had largely failed. OK, I'd been chatted up by a number of women at gigs, but that number was none.

So overall, my fantasy bubble had been burst by the grim reality that comedy was actually, thus far, a bit rubbish. I was loving it, of course, but in the way you might love a blind dog who couldn't support or feed itself, and spent most of the time sitting alone by the fire, trumping uncontrollably. I still had no job, no income, and was living at home with my Mum and Dad, feeling like a financial invalid. Even living rent-free and contributing diddly squat to bills saw me make a monthly net loss, and Mum was regularly slipping me petrol money to keep me afloat.

However, I had booked myself into a number of national competitions to be held down in London, and was excited about venturing into "the Smoke" for what felt like a shot at the big time.

Before that I had other gigs booked in with some promoters I'd not worked with before. Within the first week of February, I travelled east to The Caper Club in Sheffield, north-east to Peter Vincent's Stockton Arc gig, and then back down to Stoke and along the A50 for a Spiky Mike gig in Leicester. All sets were between five and ten minutes, all were unpaid and left me out of pocket, but all went well or very well. I even got my first usable quote.

Anthony J. Brown, who runs the Caper Club, had been very effusive about my short set, and so I took the liberty of emailing him for something to put on my CV. So far my résumé read: "Done a few gigs. Almost got paid once. Better than Mick from Crewe." I could really do with a couple of extra credits. Within minutes of me shooting off an email to Anthony, he fired one back. I still have it saved in my Hotmail archives. It read:

> Hello Sir,
>> Top work last night. Anyway…
>> "Pleasingly skewed anecdotes, with an instantly likeable onstage demeanour."
>> Any use?
>> AB

My reply simply read:

> Every use! Thanks…

I'm happy to say I was never tempted to put "'Very funny' – his Mum" on the CV. I've seen comedy portfolios with that listed as a quote, and while you might think it's endearing, it makes you look like a big twonker. (I'm aware I've used the word "twonker" twice in the space of a few paragraphs, but it's my new favourite word – in your face, "lagoon".) The only thing less likely to get you work than citing your own family would be something like:

The whole crowd related to him and we all had a great laugh. We'll definitely be getting him back for our next rally.

Mr White, Grand Wizard, KKK

Everyone, the adage goes, lies on their CV. This can be especially true, I posit, for people in the Arts. The problem with venturing into something non-academic – like acting or comedy – is that the X number of years you've spent in academia instantly loses its worth. I've never once been booked for a gig because of my "A" grade for GCSE Dual Science. Nor has a promoter ever offered me a spot based on my ability to correctly employ the subjunctive tense; were that ever to happen, it would be a major shock. When you enter the Arts, you literally go back to square one – regardless of how well you administer hyperbole.

This is why you see a lot of comics inventing quotes for their repertoires. With so many comedians around, and with so few gigs to share between them, being the proud owner of a stand-out CV can make a big difference to your career, and open doors for you that remain closed to comics with less-endowed résumés.

A common practice amongst comedians is to bend rather than break the rules. So most acts won't strictly fabricate a quote, but will simply preen a review for the choicest pickings. For example, a reviewer might describe you as "a great lump of a comic, unable to make original jokes, who leaves the audience wanting something more substantial." The words should be seen, not as the final dish, but as mere ingredients. If you reduce them down to the positive words alone, you get "a great... comic... original jokes... leaves the audience wanting more..." Finally, blitzing them up together and adding grammatical seasoning, you are left with: "A great comic! Leaves the audience wanting more!"
Delicious!

It can obviously be taken to greater extremes than this. At the

Edinburgh Festival, which doesn't feature in this book because I wasn't there, all reviews follow the 1–5 star rating. It has become fashionable for shows receiving 1/5 stars to appear on the flyers as "A star!"

(For the record, my favourite example of manipulation is of a comedian who had formed part of a school choir that featured on *Blue Peter* in the late 1980s. Twenty years later, his CV read "Performed on primetime BBC1". Lovely.)

But referencing your Mum, or stating that "all my mates laugh at me" is destructive rather than constructive, as is "'Brilliant' – a punter at a gig." This is why I was overjoyed to have a bona fide quote to include in the portfolio.

I was hoping that the upcoming competitions would allow me to add additional credits to the CV. While new-act competitions don't lead to unceasing exposure and bookings, they do make for lovely epithets on a comedy CV and create a nice wave of coverage for you to surf along on for a few months.

The first of these competitions was The Amused Moose down in London. The Amused Moose has acted as a springboard for multiple big names, with previous finalists including Jimmy Carr, Rhod Gilbert, Karen Taylor and Rob Deering. My heat, I had been informed via email, would be in central London, and so, rather than drive down into the world's biggest car park, I booked a train.

***

There was a special offer on with The Trainline, and so, like a grotesque diva, I travelled First Class. It was another new experience, and it was scary and exciting – like paintballing nude. (NB: I've never done that.)

I'd always seen going First Class as the pinnacle of domestic travel, and so I'd been looking forward to the experience with baited tenterhooks. Ultimately, though, I found it to be a hideous anticlimax – like the career of Michael Owen. (I promise that's the last time I'll mention him.)

In essence, what differentiates First from Standard Class is that you have slightly more leg room and don't have to sit next to people who smell of prison – and that's it. Don't misunderstand me, there's joy in those factors, but my mind being what it is, I suppose I was envisaging something more. In my head, I pictured myself boarding the train to be met by a league of merry dwarves holding brimming tankards of mead and platters of fresh meat. Instead, I got a woman named Gill with a glass eye and a trolley. There wasn't even a special toilet. I had expected, as a bare minimum, to have some kind of scaled-down orchestra playing softly in the corner of a private lavatory, but instead I was forced to share with the rest of the proletariat – everyone hoping they could hold it in until they reached their terminus. After all, going to the toilet on a tilting train can be scary and dangerous – like paintballing nude with Michael Owen. (NB: I'm not sure what happened to that analogy. It started poorly and slid inexorably downhill. Oh well, too late to change it now.)

In spite of the unforeseen drab normality of journeying with the so-called elite, I still felt out of place. I hadn't planned for such an advanced level of sartorial elegance, and whereas everyone else was wearing tailored suits and burnished shoes, I was dressed like Niko Bellic from *Grand Theft Auto IV*.[7]

Travelling on a train is boring. It's a bit like being in detention at school, but instead of writing "I must not feed chalk to the fat kid" over and over, you are forced to feel mildly sick for the whole time. I spent the first half an hour of the journey wading through my subconscious. Horatio (the name I attach to my subconscious)

---

7   If you've played *GTA IV*, you will have smiled at that. If you haven't, you probably feel a little empty.

had posed the question of how I would go about taking revenge on an Eskimo. Now, I'm aware it's not an important question, nor a scenario that is ever likely to arise organically from my life in the suburbs of a Staffordshire mining town. However, this is what happens to my mind when left to its own devices, and for some reason I was unable to focus my mind on anything else for the next thirty minutes. At length, I even worked out that exacting revenge on an Eskimo would be relatively effortless – all you would need is his postcode and a can of de-icer.

Blessedly, just after we passed through Wolverhampton, I was winched from the depths of my subconscious by a ray of hope in the drudgery. The man sitting in front of me was playing Championship Manager on his laptop. It promised to be a long and uneventful journey, so after a while I started watching from behind. After about an hour I was really getting into it, looking on attentively as he battled for survival with Bristol Rovers. He was entirely oblivious to my engagement... until a last-minute equalizer for his side elicited a massive "Get in!" from the seat behind. I came clean about my actions, after which he appointed me assistant manager and made me sit beside him.

The surfacing of something exciting on an otherwise dull journey caused quite a stir in the carriage, and slowly but surely more and more people began taking an interest in this man's managerial career. Before too long, most of our fellow First Class travellers were avidly engaged in the game. The nature of a train carriage makes it very difficult for more than two or three people to look at one screen, but I humbly took on the role of "verbal vidiprinter", offering minute-by-minute commentary on the matches and giving score updates from other important fixtures. It was one of the most bizarre and joyous experiences I've ever had, marred only slightly by an elderly woman chanting "You're gonna win **** all!" from the other end of the coach. (I found out later that she was a Bristol City fan.)

***

There were eight acts on the bill that night, and the room was so small that we weren't actually allowed in to watch any of the other competitors. We all just had to wait in the wings, listening intently through the door and walls, wincing every time we heard a big laugh.

That's right – we all wanted each other to fail.

Competitions are a strange and unsavoury feature of the comedy circuit. Aside from the awards given out at the end of major Festivals – Edinburgh, Leicester, Brighton etc. – almost every comedy contest on offer is open exclusively to fresh-faced up-and-comers. And, I would say, the majority of greenhorns enter at least one competition in their first couple of years of comedy – most enter four or more, and I've known of people doing only comps in their opening twelve months.

But what competitions can do is to engender and perpetuate an unhealthy dynamic amongst performers, whereby you end up praying for the demise of your fellow showmen. It's a dynamic that doesn't exist to anywhere near the same extent on the circuit as a whole.

Sorry to break the illusion – if you were under it – but by the time you drag yourself out of the open-spot gutter and onto the comedy circuit proper, almost everyone is lovely to everyone else. It took me by surprise, too!

I always imagined comics to be a bitter, depressive bunch, sitting hunched in the Green Room cursing under their breath as their peers raised the roof on stage. Having worked briefly in sales, I suspected pro comics might be like competing salesmen: brash and flash and charming on the outside; bitter and broken and empty on the inside. But that's just not true. Comedy shares interpersonal properties with any job that involves an element of danger. It's more like being a fireman in that respect. Fellow mirth-givers tend to have a healthy respect for one another's ability to go on stage and take on a blazing crowd. And on nights when an audience refuses to be tamed, you can find real camaraderie in your co-gagsters.

That's not to say that bitterness, bitchiness and vehement despisal don't exist anywhere within the realm of professional stand-up comedy. Of course they do, but nowhere near as much as you might think. Among the rank and file, however, the archetypal view of comedians as back-stabbing jealots is much more justified – and largely because of the enforced rivalry of contests such as this.

It's almost impossible to avoid. Nobody enters a competition without having some hope of taking the title; nobody thinks, "I hope I don't do very well here." Everybody wants to win. And everybody has moments in the run-up to the gig, no matter how fleeting, where they imagine Frank Skinner handing them an award and saying, "That was some of the best comedy I've ever seen – let's get Falafel."

But for that to happen – in order for you to win – you need everyone else in the running to do worse than you.

As I mingled with the seven other hopefuls before the show, we probed each other for signs of weakness.

"How many gigs have you done?"

"You got an agent?"

"What's the biggest venue you've played?"

"Who is Kaiser Soze?!"

A couple of the acts were playing ostentatious mind-games, bigging themselves up to the max and name-dropping at every given opportunity.

"Yeah, I was at Jongleurs the other day and I was saying to Lee – Lee Mack – that Off the Kerb [a comedy agency] want to come and watch me perform."

One lad didn't even need a proper segue.

Me: "Hello."

Twonker: "I said the very same thing to Michael – Michael MacIntyre – when I met him at the Comedy Store last week."

While it was transparently alpha-male posturing, it did make me feel slightly jittery. I'd not been down to London before, and the size of the place was intimidating. When I first drove to Manchester in October for Beat the Frog, I'd felt slightly overwhelmed by its history, its culture and its sheer size – as though I was being measured against the city as a whole. That feeling was now magnified monstrously, and the name-dropping, brown-nosing and being-a-twonkering was doing its job.

I was drawn to go on seventh out of eight. Your position in the line-up can be crucial to your chances of making it through. Like in the 400 metres, nobody wants to get drawn in lane 1 or 8. Go on first, and the audience are cold; go on last, they're ready to leave. Seventh wasn't worst-case scenario, although it meant having to sit listening to six other comedians, cringing every time they raised a laugh; smiling every time they failed to. All eight of us had paid lip-service to the idea of charity, declaring in unison beforehand, "May the best man, lady or transvestite win." This axiom lasted about as long as it took for me to work out that the man in a wig and a skirt method acting as a lady was… well, a man in a wig and a skirt.

The first two acts got very little response. The third act, or "Tranfastic", as s/he was called, started off really well, drawing cheers and laughter from all sections of the crowd. When it became clear, however, that s/he wasn't a Journey tribute act and was, instead, nothing more than a man trying to be a woman, the crowd stopped believing. Clumping off stage in heeled shoes, s/he mumbled something about the judges not knowing talent if it slapped them with unusually big hands for a lady, then pranced off into the Soho night, looking like a hideous pirate. I have no strong feelings either way about cross-dressing, but you know you've failed as a transvestite when you look uncannily like a pirate. I suppose the reverse may also be true – that you know you've failed as a pirate if…

Acts number four and five did fairly well, but nothing more. And every time an act came off stage, looking despondent and kicking the skirting-board, the voice in my head cracked open another beer and started singing, "Delilah".

Then act number six went on. The only woman on the bill, she had been the least brash and outspoken about her achievements on the comedy circuit. With a soft, mellifluous Geordie accent, she had fooled me into thinking she posed no threat. She just seemed like a very pleasant, very harmless lady. Then she went on stage. The rest of us gave up hope.

Her name was Sarah Millican.

She destroyed that room like fat-fighters in a gingerbread house. Every few seconds, we would hear a laugh, then another, then a round of applause. The flimsy panelling in the hallway even shook with the force of the response. My face contorted. My inner monologue took a revolver and locked himself in the study. Where Tranfastic had failed, Sarah had succeeded in two major areas. First, her boobs weren't from Ikea. Second, she was really, really funny.

I went on straight after her and, in fairness, did very well. I got laughs in all the right places and my "blocking" and stage-craft were solid. But it wasn't good enough – how could it be?

As we all stood there at the end, waiting for the result, I realized what it must be like to represent the Green Party on election night. You stand there putting on a brave face, but inwardly you know you'd have been better off staying at home and sorting out your recycling.

The journey back was marked by despair and bitterness, and it had nothing to do with the failure of Bristol Rovers to make the play-offs.

***

There was a minor saving grace to the evening, and it came in the shape of my Mum. In times of hurt, I've always been able to rely on her to make me feel better, and this time was no different – albeit inadvertently.

The taxi I'd taken from Stoke Station dropped me outside Mum and Dad's house just after 2.30 a.m. Feeling exhausted and disconsolate, I lumbered into the house and made for the kitchen.

I'll have a hot chocolate and a block of cheese. That'll take the edge off the despair.

Merely instants after I'd flicked the switch on the kettle, a loud thud reverberated around the house. This thud was swiftly followed by a hasty *pad pad pad* as my dear mother – startled by the late-night disturbance – shot out of her bed and raced to the top of the stairs. Failing to mask the panic in her voice, she called down:

"Andrew, is that you?!"

"Yes, Mum – of course it's me!"

Then my Mum came out with a sentence I'm fairly confident nobody else has ever used.

"Oh, thank goodness for that – I heard the kettle, I thought it was burglars!"

Burglars?!

Even if we neglect the fact that Mum knew to expect me back late – and that on every other gig night, I'd arrived home in the small hours – that still doesn't answer the more pressing question: Who breaks into a house and brews up?!

"Dave, you get the DVD player… I'll make you a mocha."

Still, I can always rely on Mum to lift my spirits, and lumping off a mammoth hunk of cheese from the newly opened Cathedral City, I went to bed feeling altogether more cheered. And then, predictably, I had nightmares.

***

"How did it go?" asked Dad hopefully. It was the next morning and I was mournfully eating my way through a bowl of Cinnamon Grahams.

"It went pretty well, yeah – I came second."

"So what does that mean – is there a next stage?"

"Yeah. I'm going down to London again next week."

Both of those statements were true, but one didn't follow logically from the other. There was a next stage, and I was going down to London again in a few days, but for another competition – one that I hadn't already been eliminated from. However, the fallacy of affirming the consequent was a small price to pay for keeping my Dad from the truth.

It was over a month since Dad had asked about my job search. I hadn't looked for a job, and had, in lieu, been searching for the hero inside myself and trying to slot cheesy nineties song lyrics into all my sentences. I had hoped that the "paid gig" in Crewe and the advent of a few talent contests would help me to push it, push it real good towards "making it". As we all know, the "paid gig" remained unpaid, and with people like Sarah Millican around to shine like a star, I sensed the chances of me winning any kind of contest with "comedy" in the title were about as high as the chances of a man with no hands suddenly having hands.

In all seriousness, how could I tell Dad that since we last spoke, I had actually lost money? How could I tell him that the gigs I'd done in Sheffield, Stockton and Leicester weren't, contrary to what I'd insinuated, paying any kind of fee? How could I tell him that the savings with which I was paying for travel were scraping the barrel's bottom, and that the £20 he thought I had made from gigging in Crewe was now the amount I needed to borrow from Steve to get back down to London?

It wasn't that he wouldn't have helped me out financially. Of course he would – he had been doing just that for over two decades. It was simply that I wasn't ready to give up yet. If I could persuade him that I was doing well, maybe it would give me time to persuade the world of comedy. For as long as my hope held, I could, with any luck, suspend his.

If this was just a moralistic story, I wouldn't include this part. I wouldn't concede that I lied to my own Dad; that I was scared to let him think I was failing; that there was a growing unspoken tension in the house. I'd make him say things like, "Follow your heart, son!" and "Do what you love doing!" But again, this story is real. It was a painful time.

The fact that my Dad was keeping his side of the bargain by trying to be supportive and not pressurizing me into seeking pastures new made the predicament worse. I wasn't keeping my side of the bargain – the side that would see me making any kind of discernible progress, or any discernible cash. So I kept fibbing. I kept fibbing and I kept praying that I wouldn't always have to. I was living a lie, but I was relying mightily on the Truth.

***

It was with suitably attenuated hopes that I re-embarked on the road to London, for my next attempt at comedic salvation: The Laughing Horse New Act Competition.

The Laughing Horse is, I think anyway, the most highly subscribed of all the competitions, with about 800 hopefuls entering that year. The contest is split up into four rounds – heats, quarter-finals, semi-finals and, yes that's right, the Final. All of the heats that year were held down in the capital, although more recently they have held some further north – in Nuneaton and Leicester, for example.

I had been informed that the qualifiers from the early rounds would be decided by audience voting. It would therefore make sense to try to recruit some friends to come along. All my London-based friends were fictional and set in Victorian times, so I feared they might not be able to make it along. Instead, I turned to my trusty steed… sorry, Steve. Along with him, I also managed to convince one of my few other genuine friends, Big Dave, to accompany me to the gig. Dave agreed on one proviso – we could go and watch Stoke City. So with the bloke from Stoke and the… er… twanger from Bangor, we made haste for Londinium.

Dave's beloved Stoke were away at Crystal Palace, and, I Google-mapped, we could get from their Selhurst Park ground to Kingston in plenty of time for the gig, so I happily concurred with the plan. Dave was well up for the whole thing, and I think he hoped we'd be able to muscle into another mobile game of Championship Manager, "although I don't wanna be Bristol Rovers – we'll have to make 'em be Stoke," he insisted.

Ironically, we did get muscled into a football-related train incident, but it wasn't so much a management simulation as a beat 'em up.

The cross-country train we took down to London was largely uneventful on this occasion. I spent the time running through my set-list and trying to think of jokes that would ingratiate me with a city audience. Steve tried to help by intermittently telling me about this girl he'd met, called Erin, and how, despite a nine-year age gap and a distinct lack of interest from her side, he was planning to marry her. Dave found nobody playing Championship Manager, but he did find a few other Stoke fans and they ended up chanting us into the capital with songs about how Stoke were the best football team the world has ever seen – songs, I might add, that were evidentially unsubstantiated and full of logical fallacies.

By the time we got on the tube, though, we had lost track of Dave's fellow Stoke fans and found ourselves in an empty carriage to ourselves. An empty carriage, that is, until we reached Waterloo and the carriage doors opened to reveal nine (*nine!*) Millwall fans. Bustling onto the train, I noticed three very obvious things about them. Firstly, they all had massive biceps that were barely contained by their blue Millwall shirts; secondly, with tattoos sporting the phrase "Buccaneers" (Millwall's hooligan firm), and faces resembling hastily made Toby Jugs, they looked like they enjoyed a bit of bovver. Thirdly, they were all staring at Dave.

Steve and I, not being Stoke fans, were in normal civvies, but there was no hiding the red-and-white Stoke shirt in which Dave was bedecked – and, seemingly, about to be decked.

You don't have to know much about football hooliganism to understand that Millwall's Buccaneers are renowned as some of the worst. A little bit more knowledge, and you will learn that Millwall hate Stoke, and Stoke hate Millwall. So this scenario was far from ideal, and was, in fact, a massive shame.

Scenting their prey, all nine of the blue-shirted Millwall fans came and sat surrounding Dave, Steve and I – some arrayed on the seats opposite, some squeezed up next to us. Steve and I sat there as all nine of them proceeded to make threatening remarks to Dave – none of which are suitable for broadcast – as well as making gestures and gesticulations which carried a non-too-subtle message: Dave was dead.

I was, in all seriousness, the most petrified I have ever been. I sat there, trying to hide my trembling, thinking to myself, "Is my friend about to be murdered in front of me? And more importantly, can I run in flip-flops?"

The tension and fear amongst the three of us was palpable, almost debilitating. Dave is a big man and knows how to handle himself, but against nine thugs he had little chance. Steve and I would have little chance of protecting him if it did kick off. I'd watched *The Football Factory* and *ID* and *Britain's Worst Hooligans*, but never expected to be featured in a re-enactment. I'd always hoped, if I were to be in a film reconstruction, that it would be *West Side Story*.

Then Horatio, the voice in my head, decided to break the silence. "Why don't you say something, Andy?" he whispered. "It will be helpful, I promise."

So, without really wanting or expecting to, my mouth opened and the following words flowed out: "Is there any chance we can defuse this with a dance off?"

"Oh, you want some too, do ya?" one gentleman enquired.

Oh thanks, Horatio! Another fine mess you've got me into.

This was the worst thing ever. I always thought I'd get assassinated in my early fifties, but it seemed I didn't even have that to look forward to. The chunting of the train as it made its way along the track only heightened the sense of tension.

Sometimes in life, though, you get what I call "redemption moments"; points in time where a dire situation gets defused by an invasive instant of hope. I'm delighted to say, this was one of those times. Slightly farther down the carriage was a five-year-old boy sitting with his mother. Gazing around the train, he noticed Dave in his red-and-white vertical-striped Stoke shirt, surrounded and swamped by a sea of blue Millwall fans. Excitedly turning to his Mum, this five-year-old hero proclaimed quite audibly:

"Mummy, look – I've found Wally!"

All the Millwall fans looked over to the young man, then looked back to Dave. Then, miraculously, as one, they all started laughing.

"Fair play, that is quite funny."

"Go on, have a good day, mate. Who you got – Palace?"

"Uh-huh," Dave managed.

The train pulled into the next station.

"Stuff 'em for us, geez. Have a good 'un."

And they all got off, chuckling to themselves and saluting the young child who, without knowing or caring, had saved three very grateful, very flatulent men from one hell of a kicking.

I remember Jasper Carrott once saying about writing material, "Just observe what happens to you." I took that on board that night, once more deciding to employ the autobiographical touch and recount the day's events. It had worked in the aftermath of the Witches' Coven catastrophe, and it worked again here. I went on second this time, after a pretty shoddy first act who had been heckled mercilessly by Steve and Dave.

I opened with the tube story – the genuine fear with which I retold it adding a visceral authenticity. There were twelve acts on the bill that night, and perhaps that number again in punters, but the modest crowd lapped it up and it helped me set my stall out early on – a stall on which I then arrayed my more tried and tested material. I ripped the roof off, receiving a round of applause on two occasions – for the "I found Wally" bit and for the "unicorn fillets" line in *Ready Steady Cook*. My belief that it had gone down a storm was confirmed when, on returning to the corner of the room where all the acts were standing, all of them looked livid and the first act was already leaving. Even Sarah Millican, I fancied, might struggle to follow that – which was a moot point, given that she'd already won her heat.

Overall, the standard that night was pretty good – aside from one bloke called Matt Haydock, who had apparently been gigging for five years and had never risen above the level of "Please God, make him stop – his jokes burn my eyes."

Sadly, Steve and Dave weren't there to see me crowned as the winner – they were ejected during the second half for verbally abusing every single act that wasn't me. In their defence, only one of the acts had started crying, but then if you try stand-up at sixteen you're asking for trouble. I found them in the pub next door, playing Kabadee, downing shots of whisky and having a lovely time, far from the reaches of anything in a Millwall shirt. As the phrase goes, what doesn't kill you makes you drunker.

Sitting in Nandos as we waited for our train, I fired off a text to Victor: "I'm through!"

My phone pinged twenty seconds later: "Me too!"

It felt good to be into the next round; really good. I'd played a blinder, and now I needed an easy draw for the Quarters.

And I still needed a paid gig.

And now for a full classified check:

Andy Kind 1	London 1
Nandos 0	Steve 3
Crystal Palace 2	Stoke City 0

Big Dave v Millwall Fans: match postponed.

March

I was halfway through my first year in comedy. Sitting with my diary open in front of me, flicking reflectively through the pages, I smiled nostalgically as, on turning back to September, I found "STAND-UP COMEDY GIG IN BATH – OO-ER MISSUS!" written using unnecessarily camp terminology.

Was I happy with the way the last six months had panned out? "Yes and no" was the disappointingly vague answer.

At brass tacks, I had failed to make any money from comedy and had experienced terror and uncertainty like at no other time in my life. Furthermore, my relationship with my parents was strained, my graduate degree was depreciating fast and the closest thing I had to a girlfriend was Steve.

But I had also had a lot of fun. I'd done plenty of gigs, received a lot of laughs and, most importantly, I was still going. Word had got around amongst promoters that I was "one to watch" – a good, solid new act who wouldn't let you down over ten minutes.

I was through to the next round of a competition, was getting better all the time and was enjoying gigging immensely. If you'd offered me that at the start of September, I would have taken it.

Actually, no I wouldn't – that doesn't begin to be accurate. And this, I mused, was where the main lesson had been learned. Like every foolish upstart who wants to follow their dream but has no real inkling into its viability, I had assumed back in the autumn that if I was still going by the summer, then it would mean I'd made it.

After six months on the circuit, I had predicted, I'd be gigging every night, winning awards, flirting with TV execs and living in my own pad where I could watch *Baywatch* in peace and not induce maternal heart-attacks by coming home late. I certainly didn't expect to find myself hundreds of pounds down, still without a paid gig and still – I noted, leafing forward through the diary – with gaping holes in my schedule. If someone had imparted to me back in September that after nearly thirty weeks of doing comedy, all I'd have to show for it was a few extra friends on MySpace and some strongly worded letters from the bank, I wouldn't have bothered starting. Nobody would put themselves through the anxiety of live performance if they knew that the only thing to be classed as "outstanding" would be their student loan repayments.

But here's where the change had taken place. As I sat there in my increasingly tatty tracksuit, there was now no chance of going back. I'd gone too far (well, Wisbech) to turn tail and retreat. Outwardly the signs of success may not have been on show, but inwardly I felt different. *I felt like a comedian.* Now, when I arrived at gigs, I didn't automatically turn to jelly and wobble into the venue. I could get on stage and feel comfortable; in fact, there were days and weeks where I only felt comfortable on stage. I was getting up in the morning and writing new material. Yes, a lot of it was worse than Third World debt, but I had never invested so much time in anything else, *Baywatch* and Championship Manager notwithstanding.

Above all, I had realized that doing a handful of stand-up routines isn't a quick-fix, sure-fire route to superstardom. I was now acutely aware, where I hadn't been before, that turning pro requires a lot of time in the trenches. Beyond that, I understood that my previously blinkered view of comedy as an outsider was just that – blinkered – and that I was doing as well after six months as most people who had gone on to turn professional.

Harry Hill, by his own admission, didn't get a single laugh in his first year, and a member of the audience coughing was seen as a sign of support. Furthermore, comedy legend Eddie Izzard used to be utterly dreadful in his early stages, while Jack Dee famously almost gave up at one stage, he was faring so poorly. But they kept going, and so would I.

The axiom that comics are born rather than made is a myth. Being funny may be an innate talent, but engaging an audience, structuring a joke and captivating a collective imagination is all about craft. It's not like *X-Factor*, where within the space of a few short months, an undiscovered talent can be catapulted into the national limelight. With comedy, it really is 90 per cent perspiration and 10 per cent inspiration.

The idea that one good gig makes you a supreme entertainer had been suitably dispatched from my thinking – as had the notion that being that funny mate down the pub was enough to see you through.

All of my past misapprehensions had served as rites of passage – fantasies that needed to be dispelled before any real progress could be made.

If pop stars are like fast food or microwave meals, a top comedian is like a fine wine – it takes years to achieve full flavour. But one thing was for certain: I was maturing.

And then the paid gig came.

Pipe smokers will tell you that a good smoke requires two stages of ignition – a false light and a true light. The false light comes first, expelling any extra moisture from the tobacco and preparing it for the true light. Without the false light, the true light would not be possible.

Toby Hadoke, who had compèred Cheeky Monkey back in October, rang up out of the blue.

"Hi, Andy. Been hearing good things about you. And Wayne Williams was saying that you never got paid at a gig you were doing for him?"

"Yeah, it was a bit annoying but I got some material out of it."

"Anyway, I run a gig called XS Malarkey in Fallowfield [Manchester]. We've had a drop-out for next month and I wondered whether you'd be free to do our fifteen-min support slot. It's £30."

"That would be awesome, Toby. Thanks."

"It's a bit like in pipe-smoking, I suppose, where—"

"Yeah, I've got that covered, thanks."

I made that last bit up.

This was great news. I was about to go and tell Dad, when the phone went again. You know what they say about buses? Don't let your Gran drive one.

"Kindy, Kindy, Kindy!"

It was Tony Vino. We'd been in email contact since the YMCA gig at Christmas, and I had revised my opinion of him. I still had no reason to believe he was anything other than a cripplingly bad comic, but as a human being he was simply delightful, and had been very supportive electronically about my attempt to make a career out of comedy. (And when I say "supportive electronically", I simply mean that the emails he sent were encouraging – not that he posted me a toaster.)

"Hey man. Do you fancy doing a paid gig in a church?"

"Er… sure."

"Great, it's in Blackburn. The lady organizing it will be in touch. Have a good 'un. Byeeee."

Hello, Mr Bigtime! Horatio pitched in.

This is where this story diverges from the standard "everyman comic" narrative. Everyone does bizarre gigs in crazy locations during their first year in stand-up. I've known of comics who have performed at bus-tops, on patios, in the middle of fields, and, in extreme cases, Huddersfield. But few dare venture into the perceived comedy graveyard of a church hall. In fact, I don't know many comedians at any level who would give serious credence to performing to a group of Christians – either through fear or some personal ethical stance. And frankly, who can blame them?

Andy Kind, though, is different. I laugh in the face of fear; I scoff at ethics; I needed the cash. I also thought that being a Christian myself would inspire an instant bond between myself and the expectant ranks of the faithful. Haha.

Now, I would never want to be accused of libellous comments, so we will simply refer to the church as St S*v*o*r's. Yes, I don't think you'll crack that code.

Before we get to Blackburn though, let's reverse to 2003. Time for some more backstory – here comes the science…

***

I became a Christian shortly after University. I'd always believed there was someone out there bigger than me, but concluded it was probably Luciano Pavarotti. Then, at University, I acted like lots of students act: I drank too much and behaved as though I'd never heard of STDs.

It wasn't that I didn't have thoughts or questions about God and Faith during my stint at Warwick. It was more that, as a dedicated student, there were always more pressing questions to answer, such as "What flavour pot noodle should I have for my tea?", "Who's my favourite Chuckle Brother?" and above all, "Should I wash my sheets this week or just Febreze them again?" Ultimately, I just… didn't… care.

In those days, I would always refer to myself in conversation as a Christian – often on the same nights where I would get so hammered, that other punters could get passively drunk just by being in the same room. *The Warwick Boar* (a student rag) once ran a front-page story that a string of female students had been the victim of drink-spiking. It caused havoc on campus and even made the local mainstream press. That in itself, of course, is not funny. But there is an outside chance that there was no such spiking and that the poor unfortunates just happened to be standing within thirty yards of me on an all-day-bender.

There was a lovely young lady called Ali, whom I knew socially, who was a member of the Christian Union at Warwick. She once asked me how I could claim to be a Christian when I drank to oblivion, slept around on a semi-regular basis and would occasionally hit people if I didn't like the way they were dancing. I replied that being a Christian meant believing in Jesus, and that I did believe in Him so I was a Christian.

"It doesn't work like that," she responded, fixing me with a pair of smiling eyes. "Surely a Christian *follows* Christ? If you genuinely believe that Jesus is who He says, how can that not be the single most important thing in your life? And if it isn't the single most important thing in your life, how can you claim to genuinely believe it?"

She was so gentle in what she said, and so non-judgmental – all she did was ask me a question – that I felt almost instantly guilty after I told her to **** off.

As I stormed back to my hovel that evening, I recall using words like "bigot", "self-righteous" and "hypocrite" – as well as numerous words that you won't hear before nine o'clock on the BBC. I was so angry, in fact, that the requisite pool of expletives wouldn't suffice, and so I started joining different swear-words together to form new "megaswears".

It took me nearly another two years to admit she was right.

It's a weird product of our culture, I think – and a ruined monument of Christendom: belief without action. If you believe the bowl of soup in front of you is too hot to eat, do you still take a massive spoonful to your lips? Or if you believe that *Family Guy* is the best programme on TV, do you refuse to watch it?

Jesus is either God incarnate or He's the biggest hoax/fraud/lunatic in the history of humanity. There is no middle ground. Ali, to give her credit where it's due, didn't tell me to believe the former. She just told me to make my choice – and to live out that choice. Eighteen months later, after a string of failures, heartaches and outbursts, I finally got round to asking myself that same question: Do I genuinely think Jesus is real?

The idea is a baffling one: that there is a loving God who cares profoundly about each and every human being; that in spite of our refusal to acknowledge Him, He bridged the gap between us by His incarnation, crucifixion and subsequent resurrection. I have real problems with that concept. The main problem I have is that I believe it; I believe it more than I believe anything else.

Ali was right. How can you believe in Jesus and then live as though nothing has changed? How can you treat Him like a good-luck charm or a club? The book of James tells us that "even the demons believe – and shudder." How can you possibly think that believing in Jesus and then living for your own ends is going to do you any good whatsoever? How can I?

I can't. Christ is either everything or nothing.

So I decided to stop saying things like "The Bible is a guideline" or "I try to live a good life" or "It gives me a moral code"; to stop referring to myself as an "armchair Christian" or a "non-practising Christian". All of that is vacuous b******s. Being a Christian is about being in a daily, intimate relationship with the risen Christ. I decided to stop being merely a token "believer" and to start being a "follower".

This isn't a book on theology, so I implore the theologians to forgive my rather clunking summary. Nor is it a book on apologetics, and so I hope the sceptics will not baulk at my rather impassioned discourse. I am simply concerned here with telling my story.

As I drove up into the fine county that is Lancashire, I reminisced about Ali's words: how they had lain dormant in my sub-conscious; how – if I'd only let them – they could have stopped me breaking the heart of the first girl to love me; and how a penniless Warwick student managed to drink his way through most of Eastern Europe's liquid exports in the space of four years. Unbidden, I dove hard into a sea of nostalgia, smiling at the recollection of blurry drunken nights and swimming hard towards the memory of a girl with dimples on her face.

Jess.

***

I adore the Lancashire accent. It's like being wrapped in a big blanket after playing out on a cold evening. You could tell me anything in a soft Lancashire accent – no matter how grave – and I'd receive it with a patient shrug. If I ever lose a leg and fail to notice, I want someone from Blackburn to be the one to point it out.

My paternal Grandmother was from Blackburn, and it felt somewhat appropriate that my first actual paid gig should be linked to my family tree in some way. Gandhi once paid a visit to Blackburn during his campaign to boycott British textiles, and now here I was, bringing them some material of my own. Lucky Blackburn.

Performing in a church, I realized, was not something I envisaged undertaking when I got into comedy – even though my decision to have a crack at stand-up was very much inspired by where I thought the Big Man might be leading me.
Sorry, another brief flashback. Marty, fire up the DeLorean.

I was about to apply for ordination training (i.e. I had decided to become a vicar). All the other jobs I'd tried had been a disaster, and I was struggling to find something that I (a) didn't find boring, and (b), see (a). I had a real sense that God wanted something specific from me and for me, and without any obvious alternative leads, I started to make enquiries about joining the clergy; after all, it's a safe job where you are appreciated and respected by everyone around you, the money's good and the media leaves you alone.

After Uni, I tried various jobs but none of them had worked out. During my time working for a marketing company, I used to pass the time between calls by writing comedy sketches and ideas for sitcoms. I really wanted to be a comedian, but as I've said previously, it just seemed so unlikely, even self-indulgent − after all, who gets to follow their heart's desire?

I'd briefly worked in a residential home for old people, as the entertainment co-ordinator. I do mean "briefly". After two weeks, they sacked me and closed down my Fight Club.

One Tuesday morning, as I sat watching a five-foot-high stack of comedy DVDs − laughing, analysing, deconstructing, pining − I penned a letter to a chap called Mark Geldard (not to be confused with Bob Geldoff, who has an entirely different name). Mark Geldard was Director of Ordinands for the Lichfield Anglican Diocese, and was responsible for filtering applications for ministry. Within a couple of days, he had replied and invited me to come and visit him for a chat.

Over the following couple of days, several people − none of whom knew anything about my speculative route into ministry − seemed to confirm that this was what God had planned. First of all, a friend of the family mentioned out of the blue that he thought I'd make a great preacher. A day later, at church, one of the ministry team informed me that she'd been praying for me and got a picture of me on stage, preaching. Within moments, another woman sidled up to me with a big grin on her face.

"I had a weird dream last night. I was cartwheeling up and down the street, and then I stopped to listen to you giving a talk on a big stage. How bonkers is that?"

"Totally nuts."

Just in case I hadn't got the message, I returned home to be told by my Mum that she'd asked a friend to pray for me, and within five seconds of closing his eyes the phrase "ministry" had rocketed into his consciousness.

This whole string of tightly woven events left a singularly bittersweet taste in my mouth and my soul. On the one hand, it was exciting that God was answering my cries for help and guidance; on the other, it wasn't the answer I wanted: I didn't want to be a vicar.

A round-trip to Lichfield from Newcastle-under-Lyme takes about an hour and three quarters. My meeting with Mr Geldard lasted seven minutes. Within the first six minutes I unpacked what I felt God was saying, and he listened intently. Then, taking an old burley pipe from his mouth and squinting down his spectacles at me, he said slowly, "Why shouldn't the gifts and desire that God has given you be the ones He wants you to use?" His gaze burrowed into my soul.

"You're waiting for a voice in the heavens to shout down instructions, and yet you inform me that the thing you most want to do, and the thing you think you are most gifted at, is making people laugh. The decision would seem to be unanimous, would it not?"

There was a cacophonous clanging as a thousand pennies dropped. That short speech – those sixty fleeting seconds – were like the opening of thick, velvet curtains on an August morning. *Toute de suite*, the fog lifted and the path was suddenly there in front of me. Everything became crystal clear, and the pictures and prayers and dreams of other people took on a new, transparent meaning. Maybe God really was calling me to take to the stage – not to sermonize or Bible-bash or bring chastisement, but to bring laughter, joy and healing. Maybe I genuinely could become a comedian? Maybe the creator of the universe genuinely had that planned for me? Maybe the decision was, indeed, unanimous.

"Mr Geldard, you've been a great help. Good luck with Live Aid."

So when I got the call from Vino about this church gig, you might think it would have been a no-brainer: God led me into comedy, so doing comedy in a house of God should be simple?

But I'd never heard of comedy in a church. And because I'd never heard of it, I'd never thought of trying it myself. *And will a group of Christians feel comfortable enough to laugh at stand-up?* remarked Horatio, the voice of my subconscious. *But I'm a Christian and I laugh at stand-up,* I countered. I should state at this stage that I do not have split-personality disorder. *And neither do I.*

It would be fine, I concluded. I quite like the idea of being a champion for young Christians to be inspired by. I might even meet my future wife. Horatio laughed – and not with me.

***

The venue I turned up at was less the hip, thriving church I'd hoped it would be, with lots of single young women waiting to flirt with this pioneer of Christian comedy. No. It was more like the set of *Last of the Summer Wine*.

What Tony Vino hadn't told me – either because he didn't know or because he didn't want me to – was that it wasn't a bespoke comedy night at all; it was a monthly meeting of the Mother's Union, and I was their guest speaker.

I was met at the door by a lovely old lady named Margaret, who called me "young man" about six times in the first thirty seconds – to the point where I thought she might be Harry Enfield in disguise. She led me through into the church hall "where you'll do your speech", and introduced me to the rest of the audience: five old ladies between the ages of 70 and 102. They all hit me with separate barrages of "young man" and then starting nattering amongst themselves, during which time I overheard the words "jam", "handsome" and "fresh blood".

Margaret, the youngest of the posse at 70, ushered me through into a side room which had been designated for me to prepare in. I was already nervous. On entering any venue and surveying your audience, there is always a voice in your head that asks, "Will these people laugh at you?" Here though, I was more preoccupied with the question, "What if one of them dies while I'm on stage?"

Margaret, bless her three pairs of thermal orthopaedic cotton socks, was being incredibly helpful and maternal. "You can change into your suit here, young man. We'll start in about fifteen minutes."

I didn't tell Margaret that I didn't have a suit, and that the Matalan hoody that I'd arrived in was my stage outfit of choice. Instead, once the door had been closed behind her, I checked for air-vents, secret passages and any other possible route of escape.

How is anything I have to say going to be funny to them?

Comedy is all about recognition. If you can't relate to what a comedian is saying, you won't laugh – it's as simple as that. And so comedy, in some respects and at certain times, boils down to trying to cover the largest area of middle ground with your audience. I wouldn't say that is the recipe for all comedy – or even the best comedy – but all the comics you can think of who might be described as "crowd-pleasing" are those who have mastered that technique.

So, given that laughter is about recognition, what the hell was I expecting this tiny group of old dears to recognize in my set? What were they supposed to relate to? I had zero material on Spinning Jennies or The Blitz.

Stressed and scared, I plunged head-first into the deep archives of my mind, frantically splashing around in the hope of finding any pearl of material – no matter how fishy – that I could offer these ladies; a pub joke here, a reference to *Dad's Army* there. I rang up my Gran to ask if she knew of any old jokes. She said she didn't know anyone called Andrew and hung up.

I was "contracted" to do thirty minutes – which in itself was ten minutes' worth of material more than I actually had. I was even preparing to wheel out a poem I'd written as a fifteen-year-old about a cat. It wasn't a funny poem; nor was it very good; and I couldn't remember all the words, but it still felt like my strongest material.

Some comedians I know would not go through this internal crisis. They would turn up, do their thirty minutes of pre-planned material, take the money and run. But I've always thought that was dishonest, to be honest. Churning out the same stuff night after night, regardless of who is in the crowd, I think, takes away the core of what live comedy should be – a visceral, intimate, two-sided experience where anything can happen. I see it as being like going on a first date. You may have questions you plan to ask a lady or places you intend to take her (or him, if you're a lady/homosexual), but the heart of the date is in its unfolding – the minute-by-minute interaction between the two parties, and the excitement and danger that is prevalent in that. If you're with a girl who says, after an hour or so, "I'm not having a nice time and you smell of onions," you don't disregard that and ask if she fancies coming back to yours for a hot Ribena.

In my opinion (and do bear in mind that this is the opinion of a man who drinks hot Ribena), each set, each performance should be tailored to the audience you have in front of you. As comedian Kenn Kington says, "The comic is there for the audience; not the other way round."

So with no loose air-vents available, and with a half-remembered ditty entitled "Catface the Cat", I ventured out into the church hall to meet my doting public.

It's difficult to say whether it went well or not. By minute twenty of my scheduled thirty-minute routine, four of the six women in the crowd had fallen asleep. Deciding to cut my losses, I curtailed the routine at twenty-six minutes, which brought a surprisingly robust round of applause from the two ladies still conscious. The sudden noise caused one of the sleeping ladies to jolt awake, upon which she joined in the clapping as though nothing had happened.

As had been the growing pattern with some of my gigs, I got through it.

"Young man," one of the ladies who hadn't slept through the performance confided in me as I made my way briskly to the exit. "Young man, listen to me. I'm almost entirely deaf, and I can barely see… but I really enjoyed that." To this day, at the bottom of my CV, you will find a paraphrase of that quote: "Andy Kind – perfect for anyone who has lost all of their senses."

All of what I've written about this "gig" is true, and I write it with genuine affection for the people involved. It was my first ever gig in a church, and without it I may never have set foot on a path that has led, in time, to me writing this book. So please don't think that I'm in any way poking fun at a group of lovely old ladies. However, there is another reason why this bizarre evening merits inclusion in the story…

The fee for this career-topping gig was set at £50. £20 of that went on filling up the Peugeot 106; another £3 went on service-station snacks and a carton of Ribena (unheated); an additional £2 was forked out on the on-road 24-hour parking meter. This left me, in theory, with £25 profit. That's not a lot of money, but as you know – having started this journey with me – it is still £25 more than I'd been paid at any of the past n gigs. Any kind of fee conspired to solidify my belief that I could do this as a career.

But I was wrong to believe that about this gig; wrong, too, to expect that the evening could not get any weirder. As I made my way through the polite remarks of "Thank you very, very much" and "Do come again", Margaret confided in me that the treasurer, who was responsible for signing off my cheque, was of an absent-minded disposition and had forgotten, not only to bring the cheque-book, but to actually turn up herself.

This can and does happen in comedy, and "cheque to follow" is a much less welcome phrase for artists than "cash/cheque on the night". I was midway through writing my address on the back of my set-list, insisting it wasn't a big problem, when Margaret suffered a brainwave and went shuffling off to the kitchen. Moments later, after a singular period of clanging and rustling, she reappeared, looking triumphant and holding in her hands a replacement fee: six packets of bourbon biscuits and half a Battenberg cake.

In 600+ gigs and several years since, I am still waiting for a second promoter to pay me in confectionery. However, on the plus side, I didn't set up a Fight Club. I was learning!

I finished the month with another trip back up to Manchester. I came. I saw Victor. I conquered Beat the Frog.

There was another gig for Anthony J. Brown (good), one at the Comedy Balloon (bad), and one at Pleasure Bar in Manchester (miscellaneous). Then, on the last day of March, I hopped back down to London for the next round of the Laughing Horse. My quarter-final was in Richmond (the Kingston venue was no longer usable because Steve and Dave had drunk it).

The venue smelt like a cross between old bandages and cancer, and the upstairs room where they held the comedy was the sort of place where you might expect to find a dissected corpse hidden behind the curtain. There was no Sarah Millican this time, but a man named James Branch stole the show and easily won it. He could tell he'd done well because, as he came off stage, I looked livid and failed to make eye-contact.

"Well done, James. Would you step behind this curtain for a minute?"

I went on in the second half and did pretty well, although without Steve and Dave to hamstring the other acts I felt less secure. I finished third, though, which meant I had just about scraped through. Into the Semi-Finals!

April

It was April Fool's Day and Steve rang me up to tell me my parents were dead.

"Steve, I'm actually with my parents now."

"Oh my goodness! Don't look them in the eye and edge slowly towards the door!"

"Are you drunk?"

"Little bit."

"Steve's a lunatic," I chuckled, edging slowly towards the door.

I needed to leave the house anyway – because my Mum had found me a job. And if I ever write a more depressing sentence, I'll be surprised.

Mum had bumped into an old work friend in town, who now owned a small company that helped hotels promote themselves online.

"It's only five afternoons a week, and means you can still get to all your gigs." Mum's attempt to mollify me was clear.

"Thanks, Mum – that's very thoughtful of you," I had said quiescently, before going upstairs, closing my bedroom door and shouting, "It's not fair! I hate you! It's not fair!" while crying uncontrollably – and listening to Radiohead.

Having calmed down and highly unstrung myself, I acknowledged that maybe a part-time job wouldn't be a complete compromise of my principles; after all, I had come to a point financially where the bank were making contact so often, I had to change my Facebook status to "in a relationship".

It was quite a simple role really, which involved cold-calling hotels and guest houses and offering them advertising space. The people who worked there were pleasant enough, and they were all interested to hear about my comedy exploits – although it led to a plethora of clichés being exhumed.

"Well, remember us when you're famous."

I don't know who you are now. I've literally been here an hour.

Or…

"Oh, well, you need to be a comedian to work here."

You didn't. You needed GCSE English and a polite telephone manner.

Still, I had lots to look forward to. The Laughing Horse Semi-Final was fast approaching, and making the Final would provide substantive evidence to put before my Dad – evidence that I was on my way to the top. I had gleefully told him about my progress to the Semis, thinking it might help stem the tide of doubt that his son could succeed in his chosen field. All he said was, "Nobody remembers the semi-finalists." It was a quote usually related to the FA Cup, but it was true and it ruined my day. But again, let me be absolutely clear: Dad wasn't being nasty or malicious. Nor did he want me to fail. I just don't think he could allow himself to get too excited about something that (a) he still knew very little about, and (b) still seemed like a bit of an excuse not to get a job.

I drove back up to Manchester feeling sad. I still felt like I was letting my Dad down. I was desperate to hear him say "Well done", desperate for him to feel the same level of pride at my comedic attainments as he had done for my academic ones. But I wasn't there yet. Two paid gigs does not a career make.

Unbeknownst to both my Dad and I, a vicious circle had formed. I wanted my Dad to encourage me in what I did – to take a positive interest. But I also wanted him to see me at my best. Knowing that I was far from reaching the pinnacle of my comedic abilities, I shut him out – stopped telling him about my gigs so that he couldn't hear bad news and suspect I was failing. But in feeling shut out, my Dad, in turn, felt hurt and so stopped asking about my gigs –

which I took as a lack of interest. What a flippin' mess.

If I had invited Dad along to the gig that night, he might have seen a glimpse of what his son could do. XS Malarkey is in Fallowfield – the student quarter of Manchester. It has been running for about fifteen years and, on more than one occasion, picked up the award for being the best comedy club in the North-West. It is run, compèred and held together by Toby Hadoke, one of the nicest men in comedy and a man who deserves a special mention if *A History of British Stand-up* ever gets penned.

Victor had ripped XS the week before, and had rung me straight after the gig to share the love.

"You'll have a lovely time, Andy. They are a lovely audience and very lenient, so even someone like you should do well." Victor and I had become firm friends by this stage, and I almost didn't mind his unwarranted insult.

There was a buzz about XS that I hadn't experienced at any other club: a kind of warm, comforting hum – the sort that might be emitted by an old professor sitting in his study, as, with cat on lap and pipe in mouth, he contentedly rumbled along with Bach on the wireless. From the moment I walked through the double doors, to be met with a beaming smile from Ros and Leanne on the ticket desk, I knew it was going to be a good night. There just seemed to be a glow of camaraderie in the building – not just amongst the many acts who congregate there on their nights off, but also between the acts on stage and the audience.

I suppose that's the legacy of having such a long-running and consistently well-run comedy night – the audience know they're in safe hands.

At XS, the regular crowd don't just expect to laugh – they know they will. You don't get that amiable feeling in many comedy club settings; in fact, you don't get it anywhere other than American studio sitcoms. And that's why XS is a wonderful club. As I strolled over barwards to get myself a beer, I half-expected to find Ted Danson perched on it, wearing a massive wig and chatting up anyone vaguely resembling a woman (though I don't include Tranfastic in that).

Before the show I mingled in the Green Room, exchanging pleasantries with the likes of Seymour Mace, Jason Cook and Jason Manford – all down-to-earth guys, all interested in who I was and what I was about; all refusing to give Victor their home address.

Victor was hoping – admirably, I might add – to set up some kind of comedians' meal to build circuit rapport, and wanted to send out personal invites to a chosen few. I suspect some of the top brass thought that if they let him have their personal details, they might wake one morning to find him sleeping in their bins.

Toby Hadoke was excited to see me and greeted me like a long-lost brother. "Have a good 'un," he said imaginatively as the theme tune from *The Muppet Show* announced the start of the evening. "I know you will."

My pre-gig nerves had stabilized somewhat after six months in comedy. I could still guarantee shredded fingernails and a smelly car, but the anticipation of a bad gig no longer set itself up as a matter of life and death. And yet, in a setting where the chances of rocking it were unusually ameliorated, I was, to use the archaic phraseology, proper bricking it.

I was unearthing a feature of performing that I hadn't legislated for: that of incorrigible self-critique. The deal with comedians is that they only ever judge a gig against their own expectations. At least when you expect a gig to be awful, and then it *is* awful, you haven't really lost anything. Contrariwise, when you expect the worst from a night but it turns out pretty well, you feel elated by comparison. But when you are expecting to re-adjust the roof or be bottom-spankingly tremendous, the only way is down.

I was suddenly starting to worry that if I was anything short of brilliant, I would look merely average within the context of the gig. My logic was tying itself in knots, and I was starting to feel dizzy. I didn't want to do badly in front of some of the North-West's finest proponents of comedy. *What if I completely bottle it? What if Jason Manford gets so big, he ends up hosting a primetime show on the BBC and cites my cringeworthy performance as one of his witty anecdotes?*

Onto this canvas of flag-waving anxiety, Toby Hadoke painted a new tranquillity. Before he introduced me onto stage, he imparted to the audience that while I was a new act, I was already making waves on the national comedy circuit. I'd never heard anyone say that previously, and the boost of confidence it gave me going on stage was phenomenal. It also lifted the audience tangibly; after all, part of the reason you go to gigs – whether music or comedy – is in the hope of discovering the next big thing. Every music fan wishes they were there at the Casbah Club when the Beatles played their first ever set. The crowd at XS had seen the prototype Jason Manford; they'd witnessed Peter Kay. They had every right to hope that Andy Kind might be the next big thing.

Crushingly, I'm still not in line to be the next big thing. But I did have a lovely time at XS.

That night in Fallowfield was the stand-out gig of my entire year. It was a night where, for the first time, *I felt like a pro*. Not just a budding amateur; not even a top-of-the-range open-spot. A proper, certified pro.

Each laugh lasted twice as long as at any other gig – to the point where I was actually able to sit back and enjoy the ride with the crowd, rather than instantly having to rev up the next gag. I even used a call-back – where one of your punch lines refers to something you've already mentioned in your set. Moreover, for the first time in my fledgling career, I successfully managed to banter (whereby you go off script in an *ad hoc* fashion and try to get laughs from the moment). A lady student in the front row had a delightfully squeaky laugh. Breaking off from my prepared spiel, I asked if she had been "quoted happy" (in reference to that famous insurance advert). The spontaneity of the comment induced an exceptionally squeaky chortle from the young lady, which sent a domino effect of laughter around the room. It felt amazing. I even used a call-back – where one of your punch lines refers to something you've already mentioned in your set.

"Good work, young man," came the fleeting feedback from Jason Manford, who is, in fact, six months my junior.

"That was sublime, Andy," gushed Toby as he jaunted into the Green Room. "Do you run your own night?"

"No, not at the moment," I confessed.

"Well, you should. For someone like you who enjoys banter, it can really develop your ad-libbing ability, as well as giving you valuable stage time."

"Thanks Toby – I might well do that."

I would run my own gig. Before that, I would drive home on cloud nine, singing show-tunes and feeling like a proper comedian. And then, the very next day, as if to prove that comedy has no rhyme or reason, I would drive all the way to Liverpool and die on my massive amateur backside.

I even used a call-back – where one of your punch lines refers to something you've already mentioned in your set.

***

By this time, the gig at the Fat Cat bar in Stoke (where I did my second gig, you remember) had stopped running due to lack of interest. It had been well populated when I gigged there, and the next couple, Wayne told me, had also produced good turn-outs. But then, rapidly and irrevocably, audiences started to decline and the gig lost its viability. People just lost interest after a while.

This can often happen when a new monthly comedy night springs up. The first two months tend to be fairly well attended, but then – unless the standard is incredibly high – the novelty starts to wear off and numbers dwindle. "It's nice for a change," often tends to be the sentiment. I've seen it happen a lot, and I've seen it happen a lot in Stoke-on-Trent.

As I stated earlier, I love my home city and I consider it to be a place full of warm, honest people – for the most part, at least. But culturally, politically and socially, as the wheel of time has kept spinning, we got caught in a crooked spoke sometime during the early seventies.

A transvestite out shopping in Stoke once made page two of a local paper, sporting the headline "Freak dresser kicks off one-man Mardi Gras".

Usually, if something doesn't include darts, house music or a massive ruck, it proves to be unsustainable in The Potteries.

Recently I was listening to my friend Lamont Howie on BBC Radio Stoke, interviewing football fans about the English Defence League[8] marches that were taking place in the city. Some people were in favour. Most, thankfully, were dead against them. But the sound byte which stuck out the most, and the one which sums up the slight head-in-the-sand nature of the area, was an interview with one staunch Stoke City fan who had clearly never heard of the right-wing movement. On being asked by Lamont what he thought of the English Defence League, he chimed:

"I dunno, mate – we're just doin' our best to stay in the Premiership."

So trying to inaugurate a vibrant, self-sustaining comedy night within this vortex was going to be a challenge. However, Toby's advice about the benefits of running my own gig seemed sound and so, unfazed by the cultural milieu, I roved the streets in search of a suitable venue.

---

8   A far-right group, which has strong roots in the Potteries.

Lady luck refused to smile initially, as most of the establishments I ventured into proved unusable – either through size, shape, or the number of mad drunks in their midst. I'm always amazed how many pubs you can walk into and instantly feel distinctly unwelcome, as if having to pour you a drink and show the slightest modicum of hospitality is a massive hassle for the people working there.

On enquiring as to the possibility of hosting a comedy night, several landlords glared at me as though I'd kidnapped their children and asked for a ransom. On the rare occasions I managed to break the ten-second barrier without being asked to leave, and started discussing how the comedy night might actually work and which comedians we might book, I stood gobsmacked several times as various publicans extolled the merits of Roy Chubby Brown and how they'd fill the place if we got him down.

"How much would it cost to book Chubbs?"

"My pride, sense of decency and, possibly, my soul," I didn't say. Instead, I just said he wasn't the sort of act we would normally look to book.

"Well, as long as there are plenty of Paki jokes, you'll have 'em in the palm of your hand in 'ere," I was told, without any sense of irony or shame.

You know when someone is *so* racist, you actually look over your shoulders to make sure you haven't gone back in time?

What I wanted to do was berate them on their narrow-minded view of what comedy was – and what the world was; to admonish them for even giving credence to the thought of inviting such bigoted, outmoded, divisive filth into their taverns. Instead, being a humungous coward who hates conflict and was too scared to take a stand, I just said, "Well, I'll see who's available," before leaving the venue to void my stomach in an alley.

Just as I was about to give up the ghost and head home, feeling guilt-induced to watch every episode of *Roots* back-to-back as a form of penance, I happened upon a pub in Newcastle-under-Lyme that I didn't even know existed. Paganly named "The Full Moon", the exterior looked like it hadn't been painted since Neil Armstrong took one small step for man. Stepping inside, I was struck full in the face by Jethro Tull. *This looks ideal…*

The venue had that glorious mustiness that is so comforting in public houses, while the painted mural of musical legends like Jimmi Hendrix and Robert Plant hinted, at least, at an appreciation of creativity. There was also a stage.

For the umpteenth time that day, I uttered my sales pitch: "How would you like to run a comedy night at this venue featuring some top comics from the North-West?"

"More than interested, mate."

"Sorry?!" I choked, wondering whether the bloke had misheard.

"It sounds good. We've been talking about getting some comedy in for a while. When can we start?"

"… Er, next week?"

And so it was that ten days later, on St George's Day, with a hastily cobbled-together line-up of comedians, and anyone I'd ever met press-ganged into coming along to spectate, I welcomed people to "Lunacy: Staffordshire's newest comedy night!"

It felt a bit like an episode of *This Is Your Life*. Various members of my family and social group were arrayed in front of the ample stage, all chatting, all smiling supportively and enthusiastically, but all displaying that oddly disingenuous smile where the lips belie the sentiment conveyed through the eyes, which was invariably, "I really hope he's funny, what if he isn't funny, I *really* hope he's funny."

Aside from half of my phonebook, "assorted randomers" had congregated on The Full Moon, including, in fact, Steven Woods (you may remember he was the legend from primary school, who slipped over in the mud and trumped in one glorious movement – it was genius).

"You probably don't remember me, Andy..."

"I do, actually – I wrote about you in the opening chapter," I didn't say.

I'd somehow managed to get the event featured in the local paper, despite the night not having any link to Phil "the Power" Taylor, Robbie Williams or Oatcakes, and thereby flagrantly breaking the bounds of the standard inclusion policy. They had, remarkably, produced a double-page spread on the new night, as well as a profile of myself, or "Staffordshire's new starlet!" as they had described me in the worst case of guesswork since Donald Rumsfeld proclaimed, "Well, they're definitely hiding them somewhere." It was a lovely article, though, and was to be found hanging in the houses of my Mum, my Gran and various local perverts.

Woodsy had seen the article and was there "to support an old mate", he affirmed, though more likely in the hope of seeing me fall on my rump for a change.

The paper had even sent a reviewer along (or, more appropriately, a work experience kid from the local college who fancied himself as Ernest Hemingway). More about him later.

I was petrified. In terms of nerves, this gig outweighed all the others. Somehow it felt like starting all over again, as though I'd never done stand-up before. At least in Bath, when I actually hadn't done it before, I knew that if it went base over apex I had the consolation of living two hours away and never having to set eyes on the same people again. And even at Fat Cats, though it had been in my home town, only Steve had been there from my social circle, and would be easily silenced with a bottle of Glenfiddich (as a gift or to the back of the head – either, really).

But if this goes badly, everyone will know. Everyone will think I'm rubbish, and they'll come up to me afterwards and say things like, "I think you're very brave" when what they really mean is "I have no words to describe how much I hate you for ruining my evening."

And my Dad!

I hadn't had the courage to invite Dad – it just seemed a bridge too far in terms of what I could cope with emotionally. Instead, I asked him to stay at home with a bottle of Glenfiddich. But Mum was there, my sister was there, my Gran was there (although she thought it was a quiz night and kept asking when the picture round was). News of how I fared would very quickly reach Daddio in dispatches.

Not only had I never run a comedy night before, and was duly concerned with all the trappings of that endeavour, but I'd never compèred before either. Attempting to do both of these things in front of so many familiar faces seemed like the worst mistake since Neville Chamberlain tried to swat away Nazism with a piece of paper.

I'd called Toby Hadoke (not a Nazi) that morning for some advice. Remarkably, in spite of the unsolicited call and the audacity of its nature (effectively, I was asking him to pass onto me for free the skills it had taken him years of investment to build up), he spent a good twenty minutes on the line, talking me through the basic tenets of compèring.

"Being a good compère is not the same as being a good act," he directed. "It's not about going up there and just churning out material. It's more like being a good referee – your job is to make sure that the acts thrive. If you end up as the star of the show, you've failed. So relax, don't worry about getting lots of laughs, and give it your all."

"Legend!"

I would give it everything; after all, I'm not one to do things by halves – which, incidentally, is why I'm no longer allowed to referee.

"Where are you all from?" I asked, generically, as I addressed the crowd.

"Is that Question 1?" Gran whispered to Mum.

Following Toby's advice to relax and not chase the laughs, I engaged in the most gentle of gentle banter, doing no more than asking where people originated and what they did for a living.

"Retired, put retired – that's an easy one."

"It's not a quiz, Mum."

I certainly wasn't getting many big laughs, but because I stayed relaxed and looked in control, the audience relaxed in turn. The psychology is that by seeing a calm presence on stage, an audience presumes that all is going to plan and they can enjoy it. It's the same principle as when a pilot speaks over the in-flight tannoy. A nervous MC instils fear into the audience that the whole night is going to be a disaster – in the same way that overhearing the pilot ask "What's that red light?" or speaking in a Birmingham accent might.

Obviously, with it being a new night, there was always going to be some chancer who thought that he'd take on the host and show himself to be a comedy genius. This happened after about seven minutes of patter, when a bloke at the bar, sitting with his back turned so he could fully appreciate the night, blurted out, "I hope it gets better or I'll be asking for a refund. £3 I paid for this."

A tense silence fell over the room. It was a harsh comment (everyone else had been smiling along), but it was out there now like a violent trump, and I had to deal with it. A pilot hitting turbulence doesn't automatically put his head between his knees and wait for impact, and a compère doesn't – mustn't – fold at the first sign of heckling. My knees threatened to buckle and the glow of seventy pairs of eyes turned my face slightly red.

Please, brain, think of something. Help, Horatio!

"You paid £3 for this, mate? With those trousers, I'm surprised you've got that level of disposable income."

Looking back, that was a dreadful put-down and I'm man enough to admit it now. But at the time it felt like genius. The key thing was that I had maintained my superficial air of calm, responded briskly and said something which was wittier than his outburst. In a situation like that, where the audience was on my side, that was all I required. The place erupted in laughter and cheers, the heckler – credit to him – accepted defeat, and the night went uphill from there. I had negotiated the turbulence and now I could switch it into cruise-control and enjoy the ride.

I brought on Lloyd Langford, who I went to Uni with and who was now doing comedy like me. He opened strongly, followed by Spiky Mike who also did well. After the break, feeling that I'd ticked the banter box, I unleashed my big guns and got big, fulsome laughs from the crowd – all of whom were biased and half of whom feature on my family tree. The night was closed by Gary Delaney who I'd managed to book for a lot less than he deserved. His barrage of top-notch one-liners switched the evening from "good" to "great", and when I asked, on rounding up the show, whether people would be back next month, even the heckler cheered and shouted, "You need to up the ticket price, mate."

"Can I buy you a drink?" asked Danni, a girl from the office where I was working.

"Do you like films with Colin Firth or have any emotionally insecure friends that my friend might be sick over?" I retorted, sensually.

"Er… no."

"Lager-shandy, please."

"Lager-shandy?"

Ten seconds in and I was already flailing.

"Yes, lager shandy… but without the shandy part… I put that in for a joke… Just a lager. In fact, I'll have a pint of raw diesel… no ice."

I was hating my part-time job that Mum had kindly hoodwinked me into doing, but Danni the graphic designer was the prettiest person ever to deride me for my drink of choice. Perhaps having a proper job wasn't all bad?

Either way, the night was a massive success. I had a prospective new girlfriend, I'd made £40 on the door, and my Gran had told me she thought I was a really talented quizmaster, "but next time, include a picture round."

As he had done at the gig where I'd first met him, Gary Delaney stayed behind after the show, shooting some pool and helping me deconstruct the night in my mind. He also regaled me with countless stories of heckles he'd witnessed over the years, as well as musings on comedy in general. Talking to Gary about comedy produces the same joy and awe that conversing with Stephen Hawking about the cosmos might – although only one of them can beat me at pool.

The next morning, as I sat at the kitchen table, tracksuit-clad and with a small roll of £5 notes on the table in front of me, Dad came in from the garden.

"Fancy a bacon sandwich, son?"

"Please, Dad."

"Your Mum and sister say it went really well last night. Looks like you made a bit of cash from it, too."

"Yeah, it was a good night, all things considered."

"Well done."

Sorry?

"Sorry?"

"Your bacon. Would you like it well done, or a bit juicy?"

"Oh. As it comes, really."

You can decide for yourself what my Dad meant with those words. I didn't ask for clarification.

***

Such are the vagaries of life as a human being, that ups follow downs as surely as Victor Smithers follows pretty ladies.

Feeling elated, triumphant and alive with joy, and praising God for His faithfulness, I floated down into Newcastle town centre later that day, chest pumped out and shoulders back, revelling in the glow of a job well done. I had illusions of being accosted every twenty yards or so by overjoyed punters from the night before, stopping me to shake my hand, telling me I'd put Stoke back on the map and that they were naming their newborn children after me.

The reality, infuriatingly, is that I'm not Ray Liotta from *Goodfellas*, and the only person who stopped me in the street was a market researcher in a bib, offering free shampoo samples in exchange for just five minutes of my time. The front cover of this book hints at why that might not have seemed like a great swap.

But it didn't matter. I was on top of the world. Gary Delaney had texted me to say, "Thanks again – look forward to gigging with you again soon. G." It was another one of those tiny, throwaway lines that open-spots use to boost their own confidence beyond its intended scope. What Gary meant when he texted "Look forward to gigging with you again soon" was unambiguously "Look forward to gigging with you again soon." What I took it to mean, however, in my needy, Gollum-like mind, was, "You're clearly a professional comic in the making and so we'll obviously be working together again – can't wait." With hindsight, there's reading between the lines and then there's writing new words between the lines and rubbing out what was originally on the lines. Such is the survival instinct of a new act.

The spring sun was subtly dispersing the morning shadows, sending wisps of evaporated moisture up into the atmosphere. Seeking out a quiet place to read the gig-review I'd picked up from the newsagent along with three Crunchies, I settled on a park bench under a big oak. Flicking through the pages, binning the job supplement that was slowing me down, I eventually turned to the page headed "Entertainment".

And rage took me.

The headline read: "Kind, but not funny – comedy night a flop."

The review perniciously and whole-heartedly ripped into every aspect of the night, acting, it seemed, as a platform for the work-experience reviewer (who will remain unnamed) to show off all the synonyms he knew for "bad". Failing to recall the name of the headline act (Gary Delaney became Gary Detorey) and managing to completely misspell the name of another (Spiky Mike being transformed into that hideous half-Irish, half-Hispanic tribute act, Spicky Mick), Mr Reviewer succeeded, nevertheless, in quoting T. S. Eliot, including a dozen metaphors and using the phrase *ad absurdum*. So, although the night was ruined, at least the editor would give him a reference.

I was, according to Ernest Heming-gay (which I very childishly still call him), "a proponent of easy, formulaic comedy – far from the realms of people like Stewart Lee."

Now, this was almost certainly true, but what was he expecting?! He paid £3 to come to a rockers' pub in suburban Staffordshire – it's not *The Now Show*. Also, knowing who Stewart Lee is doesn't automatically make you a font of comedy wisdom. You can always spot a rookie reviewer, because they all make the same allusion to people like Stewart Lee, Bill Hicks and Richard Pryor, and then compare whoever they are watching unfavourably. It's like going round for dinner at a friend's house, and saying, "Ainsley would have cooked this better."

I'd love to say that I had the grace to accept the review as just one person's opinion and take it with a pinch of salt. I didn't. I wrote him one back:

Dear He-must-not-be-named-for-legal-reasons,
    In the words of William Wordsworth: you're a d**k.
    Yours faithfully, etc.

Now, this isn't the sort of letter I would write these days. Nor do I think it was appropriate to stoop to his level and respond with such crudeness. But for the best part of a year, all I had thought about was my set – making it better, tweaking it, honing it. I was new, and I was only an amateur, but I was doing all right. And yet, in one fell swoop this bloke had reduced all of my ongoing effort to a few lines of ignorant critique for the world of North Staffordshire to devour. With almost tyrannical impunity, he decreed that my act was not worthy of anything other than scorn – despite the fact that, as I discovered, he had never been to see live comedy before.

When you work on an act over such a long period of time, you come to love it. Accordingly, having someone slate it feels like watching your infant child get punched in the face.

I lost a gig from it, too. I'd been booked to do a spot at a church in Bucknall, Staffs. It was £70 and I was looking forward to it/ needed the money. But the day after the review came out, they rang up and said they were going to book someone else. In that dim light, the letter I sent in response felt like something of a Pyrrhic victory.

I should say that I have no inherent issue with reviews or reviewers, and getting a bad review from someone doesn't make them a bad reviewer. But not setting a review within the context of time, place and subjectivity really, really does.

In recent times, I've had some great reviews and some poor ones – everyone does.

    Steve Bennett, who runs the Chortle website, reviewed me last year and was largely dismissive of my stuff. Of course, it's always a bit annoying to get a negative review, but at least with Bennett you know he has a deep knowledge of comedy, and he's not just writing blind. The same applies to people like Bruce Dessau and Kate Copstick. But to be publicly appraised by someone who had never set foot inside a comedy club was teeth-grindingly, fingernails-across-a-blackboard infuriating. The equivalent would be a famous biologist trying to answer definitively a question of metaphysics.

A reviewer should be aware of the great power s/he wields, and that with it comes great responsibility. As with compèring, if the review becomes about the reviewer and not the comic, it fails.

You may have noticed that what I'm doing here is reviewing a reviewer. Furthermore, you may now, possibly, be reviewing me reviewing a reviewer. If you are, you can do better than that – which means I'm now reviewing you reviewing me reviewing a reviewer. I need a lie down.

The upshot of the review was that my confidence took a massive dent. It's plausibly true that you're as good as your last gig. It's irrefutable that you're only as confident as your last bit of feedback. I had two gigs that weekend. One for Agraman in Hull, and one for James Cook down in Birmingham. I died spectacular deaths at them both.

Overall, my career in April mirrored the weather – variable. On occasions, the sun was out and it felt like summer was coming; on other days, I wished I'd stayed at home.

May

May started off as April had finished: strewn with disaster and personal crisis. The review of the gig at The Full Moon hadn't, thankfully, been seen by anyone else on the comedy circuit, but I still wanted to claw off my own skin every time it came to mind.

I spent hours in a darkened room, deliberating over my set, wondering how I could make it less "easy and formulaic".

Should I try to be edgy?

"Edgy, you?" exclaimed Horatio.

He was right – edgy wouldn't suit. I've never wanted to offend for the sake of offending. That's not to say it shouldn't be done in comedy, because comedy can accommodate the whole spectrum of approaches; nor does my stance against "edginess" suggest that I don't have a rebellious streak, because I do. Sometimes, when my parents were away, I might, for instance, have a bath with the door open; or go a night without brushing my teeth. So don't think I'm not out there, sticking to the man on a daily basis.

But I don't agree that the best comedy makes you think. The best comedy, for me, makes you heal.

Not that my comedy was particularly healing as spring sprang into summer. It was more like a gaping wound of brokenness and vulnerability. I did badly at gigs in Oxford, Leeds and Ipswich – a total of 500+ miles for a total of about five laughs. What made it worse was that Victor was doing really well – storming venues, getting rebooked and being offered paid gigs.

I didn't want to feel jealous. I loved Victor, thought he was a great act, and sincerely wanted him to reach the top of the profession. But I was wallowing in a hole of jittery insecurity, and the green-eyed monster was tightening his firm grip around my waist. I was jealous, and I hated it.

On top of that, the gigs I was trekking to were shambolic affairs. Open mic nights with 900 acts and no audience; venues so rough that even Steven Seagal wouldn't venture in. Truthfully, there is a small town not too far from Oxford where the names of the nightspots themselves imply the nature of the place. Along one high street, there is a Bar Brawl, a Club2Death and, worst of all, a Yates.

There was plenty in the diary, but I was like a hurdler who couldn't be bothered to lift his legs and so crashed through them all, each one more painful than the last. In my diary, I'd taken to scoring my performances out of ten, scrawling the appropriate numeral next to each gig. Whereas late March and early April had been garnished with 8's and 9's, May just looked like binary code:

May 2 – 1
May 4 – 0
May 5 – 0
May 7 – 1
May 8 – *Thundercats* marathon.

I bowed out of two more competitions – both small, both unimportant, but both adding to the mound of frustration. Ringing round promoters to try to scrounge paid gigs, I was persistently fobbed off with "I'm not booking at the moment" or "I'll bear you in mind for the future" or "For the last time, this is a butcher's."

The job was going OK, at the very least, and it meant that when I took Danni out to the pub or cinema, I didn't have to ask her for petrol money.

Danni was lovely. She liked films with Chuck Norris, none of her friends were mental, and she even agreed to a two-player game of Championship Manager. Bless her, she had no idea how to play the game and ended up selling me her best players for bargain-basement prices. Still, a win's a win.

I'd even succeeded in covering up the fact that, on two separate occasions, I accidentally called her "Jess". It wasn't my fault – she had the same dimples.

***

"Mum, Dad, I have something to tell you," I confessed.
   "Oh no!"
   "No, Dad, I'm not gay – why do I have to keep saying that?"
   All three of us were sitting around the dinner table, partaking in a cheeseboard.
   "No, I just think I might stop doing comedy."
   "..........."

I was ready to give up. I'd been moping around the house, and my parents could tell things weren't going well. I continued, "I'm just not enjoying it and it's really hard and I'm useless. I might just get in touch with Mark Geldard at Lichfield again."
   "But you can't even sing."
   "Gel-*dard*, Mum – the Director of Ordinands, remember? I might just train to be a vicar."
   Saying that out loud, giving voice to all the subconscious fears and suspicions and doubts I'd been bottling up, was like downing a jug of unsweetened prune juice – hard to swallow, but the release it produced was tangible.
   "I mean, I've done OK, but it hasn't turned out as I expected. It's one step forward, two steps back most of the time."
   I sat there, my shoulders hunched and my eyes staring out the carpet, waiting for the final nail in the coffin.

Then something happened that I did not expect.
   "Look, son," Dad began, "as you know, I've always worried that comedy might not be a long-term career solution for you, and maybe that's true."

What's happening?

"But equally, you obviously care about it, and from what your Mum says you are good at it."

He's not going to stop me from stopping, is he?

"When did you start – September? And look at all the places you've been to, and all the fun you've had."

He is, you know…

"All things considered, I haven't seen you this passionate about anything since I first took you to Highbury to watch Arsenal – remember, we lost 2–1 to Derby and you cried on my knee?"

"It was never a penalty."

"I know. Anyway, as I was saying… It may well be that you never make it professionally as a stand-up comedian. But so what? It doesn't mean you have to stop performing. Do it because you love it, not because you want to make money from it. And when the Gunners lost to Derby, did they give up? No. You've got a job, you've got a good academic record, and you've got a hobby that you really enjoy. That's more than most people."

"I don't think that's your Dad," whispered Horatio.

But it was. It was my Dad acting like a massive hero, confusing and inspiring me all at once with the most unlikely of pep-talks.

Before any Gallic soppiness could be injected into the room, he redirected the conversation towards the array of cheeses lying in front of him.

"You see, in isolation, Wensleydale is a bland cheese that can't compete with the more robust flavours of a Stilton, say. But when you add chutney," he articulated, spreading some Darlington Farm relish over his platter, "Wensleydale acts as the perfect accompaniment, complementing the chutney – whereas the Stilton just clashes, too interested in doing its own thing. Wensleydale is like the Ernie Wise of cheeses, don't you think?"

And that was it. As abruptly as it had begun, it had been submerged into a new conversation. But I heard it. I definitely heard it. My Dad thought I should carry on.

So I did.

On 13 May 1989, Arsenal lost at home to Derby County, seemingly throwing away their chances of winning the Championship after nine months of hard work. It meant they had to travel to Liverpool in their final game and win by two clear goals. Liverpool were reigning champions and hadn't lost at home by two clear goals since 1983. Looking dead and buried, but buoyed and inspired by their talismanic manager, George Graham, the Gunners didn't give up, and, despite all evidence to the contrary, pulled off one of the most dramatic smash-and-grabs in the history of sport.

On 13 May, nearly two decades later, Andy Kind looked dead and buried as a comedian, again after nine months of hard work. However, buoyed and inspired by the words of his talismanic father, Dad, he didn't give up. A week later, in a bizarre twist of fate, he travelled to Liverpool for a gig at Rawhide Raw. He didn't win by two clear goals, because that's not really possible in comedy, but it went very well.

***

Lancaster was the next stop on the Andy Kind Comedy Roadshow. I picked up Victor and a pink-haired Rainbow Bright lookalike called Hayley, and we set off in good spirits. Victor is from Lancaster, and on enquiring as to its merits, he told me, "It's close enough to Blackpool to enjoy a daytrip, but far enough away to feel superior."

"We'll come off the M6 north of Preston and take the A6 from there, I think," Victor asserted. "It's one of my favourite roads."

To be fair, it is a good road.

Everyone should have a favourite road. If you haven't, you need to stop reading now and take a long, hard look at yourself in the mirror – and then go and drive around until you've made a decision. Seriously, what have you been doing all these years? And don't try to fob me off with trite inanities like "Once you've seen one road, you've seen them all." Are you seriously suggesting that the M1 is in any way comparable to the A6 that skirts the east side of the Lake District? You've got some nerve, buster.

(Sorry, I became inordinately impassioned there.)

Maybe it's just comedians and lorry drivers – the people who spend the most time traipsing up and down the country – that can speak with such passion about the road networks. You see, it's the little games like having a favourite road and seeing how much road-kill you can spot that keep you sane on those jaunts along the nation's length and breadth.

I'm always on the lookout for a new road that might capture my heart and stake a claim for the Top 10. As I sit here writing, I have an A4 sheet pinned to my wall (Comic Sans font – let's not get over-excited), displaying the current table of contenders. Out in front at the moment is the A303 that passes Stonehenge in Wiltshire. It's a beautiful road, with cracking views and a nice array of gentle dips to keep you entertained. In terms of aesthetics, it's going to be difficult to shift that bad boy from top spot – although the A29 from Billingshurst towards Arundel in West Sussex is always there or thereabouts.

You can, of course, choose your favourite road based on personal memories or nostalgia (that is, of course, if you haven't already dowsed yourself in petrol and started making your way towards the hob after reading the last two paragraphs).

For me, purely on nostalgic grounds, the A4019 from Junction 10 of the M5 towards Cheltenham scores well, as does the A525 from Newcastle-under-Lyme towards Shropshire. Both good solid roads, let's not pretend otherwise.

Part of the reason for including this banal geekiness is simply to allow you into the mind of a travelling comedian. It's not all after-show parties and shirt signing, you know. (In fact, for me, none of it is.) Some people like to cite comedy as the new rock-n-roll, and logically assume that we spend our post-gig evenings sleeping with groupies and trashing hotel rooms. In reality, it's more likely to involve a cheese-and-bacon slice from Knutsford Services and a lonely drive along the A34 (it's a decent road, let's not hide from that fact).

The other part of the reason for mentioning this at all, is to talk about the flipside. If you have a favourite road, you almost certainly have a least favourite – a road that you despise, that you approach with trepidation and hatred; a road that you wish, unrealistically, was dead. If you live in or around London, your road nemesis is likely to be the M25. If you live farther north, there's a chance you and I share a common foe: the M6.

The M6 is an idiot. It's like that bloke at a party that no one wants to talk to. He stands in the middle of the room so you can't avoid him. He looks harmless so you try to engage him in conversation, then instantly regret it as he bores you to tears with his monotonous tone and dull outlook – and then locks onto you for the rest of the evening, refusing to let you get away and sapping your will to live. There are other roads that I hate, of course. The A57 Snake Pass might sound exciting, but is arguably the most dangerous road in Britain. How did it even get there?! Presumably, at some point in the past, some clever dick said, "I know what will look good between Manchester and Sheffield: the land of Mordor!" The fact that it constitutes the major route between those two cities is very much to my own chagrin. I mean, Sheffield is a lovely city, but I don't want to have to ring my loved ones every time I go there, saying, "Know that I loved you!"

But the M6 tops them all for me. In theory, there's something quite adventurous about traversing the British Isles, crossing county lines and circumnavigating major towns. But there is one sure-fire way to put an end to the buccaneering feel; one thing that can turn even the most mild-mannered of individuals into ravenous fiends:

the British traffic jam. And the Mflipping6 is infamous for that.

And it was a huge traffic jam on the M6 that we met on our way over to Lancaster. We sat, stationary, for forty minutes, with no clue as to what the problem was. It was so bad, people were getting out of their cars and walking around. One bloke even came and sat in our car for ten minutes.

"I knew I should have taken the A34," he rued.

"It's a good road, there's no doubt about it," I said.

Finally we started snailing along – but still at that stage where, if you get into third, it feels like a massive victory. Victor rang the promoter to say we'd be late.

"Can you take a short cut?" suggested the promoter. He was worried because I was down to compère and Victor to open, so he needed us both there for the kick-off.

"Oh, what a good idea – thanks goodness we called you. A short cut – of course!" Victor hung up before he ranted himself out of future bookings. Like Hayley and I, he was just tense. Being delayed is always annoying, but it's always helpful and reassuring to know why you're delayed. That, surely, is what those huge electronic signs on the side of the motorway are designed for? But in this case, we were simply told in big flashing letters: "Incident ahead."

What the hell does that mean? What kind of incident? This has to be the most infuriating of all road signs. At least when you see "Accident ahead", you can understand why you're wasting your life stranded on the tarmac – two or more cars have collided and it has caused a backlog which the emergency services are in the process of clearing. But what constitutes an incident? Is someone trapped down a well? Has there been a murder?

"Forget the AA lads – this is a job for Poirot."

It just seems a bit patronizing to be sitting motionless in your car, only to have a sign flash up "Queue caution", as though you needed reminding. It's signs like "Incident ahead" and "Queue caution" that make the sign "Workforce in road" seem less like a warning and more like a tip-off.

I'm sorry if I've dedicated so much time to car journeys. Actually, I'm not sorry. Comedians spend more time in their cars than they do on stage, and so it's not irrelevant to focus on it; also, it feels like therapy to be able to rant about it – so thanks.

Parking up on the first piece of available tarmac, we hurried as fast as our little legs could carry us towards the gig, cutting the start time incredibly fine. As we got within spitting distance of the door, it was flung open on its hinges and Dean, the promoter, emerged from the gloom with arms spread wide.

"Thank you – thank *you*!" he gushed, striding towards us. "You're here, it's you, you're here!"

I had the distinct feeling that Dean had watched too many films in which wounded soldiers come home from the war.

"We've been expecting you," he exclaimed, wrapping his sturdy arms around Victor's skinny frame and giving him an inordinately drawn-out hug.

"Calm down, mate – it's not *Harry Potter*," Smithers quipped, straightening his glasses.

Dean moved on to Hayley and, again, embraced her for an extended period of time. I was next and I knew it.

I hate social situations like this – where one person either joins or leaves a group and feels the need to greet/bid farewell to everyone personally. It's fine if you're first in line to say "Hi" or "Bye" and you can get it out of the way, but being last is a nightmare. You start to get nervous that you'll be the only one who doesn't get a hug, or that you'll completely mis-time the proffered high-five. And what to say in those situations where you're last to say "Cheerio"? By that stage, everyone else has bagsied "Take care", "All the best", "See you soon" and "Have a safe journey", and you realize that the salutation cupboard is bare – but, equally, that it's socially unethical to double-up with someone else. I panicked once at a party and said, "Give my love to your Mum", to a bloke whose Mum I'd never met.

Unclamping himself from Hayley and moving on to me, Dean growled, feinted a Rugby tackle, then went in for a bear hug. Just to recap, this is a guy I had never laid eyes upon before this encounter.

"It's great to be here," I wheezed. (NB: Victor had used "All right, mate?" and Hayley had opted for "Good to see you" *and* "How are you?", so really it was a choice between "It's great to be here", "It's *nice* to be here", and "How's your Mum?")

My slight obsessive/compulsiveness notwithstanding, I really warmed to Dean. Whilst I was perplexed as to why a collective "Hello" couldn't suffice, I felt quite touched that Dean could be so overwhelmed by the fact that we'd simply turned up; after all, that's usually the bare minimum when you're booked for a gig.

I wonder how he'll react when I wheel out the A-bombs?[9]

The venue was a glitzy wine bar that had the feel of an establishment trying to be something it wasn't − i.e. in London.

One thing I noticed instantly was that the venue smelt clean. It didn't have that musty, dank richness that I was growing so used to in low-level comedy nights − and that I was starting to find comfort in. Bar 69 was snazzy and fresh, but lacked character and old Irishmen swearing in the corner. That said, there was a good clump of punters present and they cheered with gusto as I was introduced onto the stage to MC.

Don't be too funny − Dean might try to get you pregnant.
"Thanks, Horatio."

I grabbed the mic, placed the stand to one side and beamed at the audience. They beamed back. *Lovely.*

---

9   "Wheeling out the A-bombs" is a figurative term some comics use for performing their best material. I didn't actually bring nuclear warheads to the gig.

"Hello, I'm Andy, your compère. It's a delight to be here."

Then it started.

"**** off!" came the shout.

"Eh?" I said, glancing around for the origin of the heckle. I couldn't find it.

"Oh well, it's good to get the first heckle out of the way. We're gonna start with a game – everyone cheer like pirates… *Aaarrggh!*… Well done, mostly pirates – a few farmers down there, too…"

"**** off, w****r!" the same voice followed up.

I didn't like this. Scouring the crowd for the hit-and-run heckler, my eyes finally rested on the person responsible.

Surely not?!

It was Dean.

What the hell is going on here? Is this a wind-up?!

"Our promoter has Tourette's, everybody," I tried to laugh it off. "Dean, are you going to heckle all night?"

"Sorry, mate. Sorry, carry on."

I was completely baffled. What was this guy doing? He had been so friendly just a matter of minutes ago, and now he was ladling me with abuse. Was he just so new to the scene, he thought that heckling was all part of the show; all part of the bonding experience? I carried on.

"We've got some great acts coming up for you tonight, but first let me tell you something about myself…"

"Gippo!!"

I flipped. I know I shouldn't have done, but I was taut and confused.

"Mate, seriously, what are you doing?! I've come from Stoke to do this gig for free *and* given a lift to two other acts, and now you're calling me a gippo?! You're the gippo – what the hell is wrong with you?! You don't heckle your own acts – it's rude, it's unprofessional and you're a b***** idiot!!"

There was, as you might imagine, an awkward silence. Then Dean spoke…

"Sorry, mate. As I say, I've got Tourette's – I thought you knew that?" His tone was pained and apologetic.

"… I… n… I didn't know that, no. I thought you were joking," I whispered in a voice that could only be described as squeaky.

"I'm sorry, mate, I didn't realize – I shouldn't have snapped at you," I continued. It had turned into an episode of *Jeremy Kyle*.

"W****r!"

It wasn't Dean this time, but another punter who had decided my outburst was unfair, and my contrite apology insubstantial.

Ha ha ha!

"Quiet, Horatio."

Seriously, though. Tourette's is a horrible condition for people to cope with, and I have huge respect for anyone who manages to negotiate it and still keep a smile on their face. But to run your own comedy night and heckle everyone you've booked seems a little counter-productive. It would be like a vegetarian opening a butcher's. A *promoter*, with *Tourette's?*

Fortunately, the crowd were, ultimately, a forgiving bunch, and the gig did pick up after the initial glitch. Dean continued to hurl impulsive abuse at everyone who went on stage, only to approach them afterward and say, "Cracking set – loved it!" He was a charming, authentic guy who seemed to love comedy, but you wouldn't let him lead prayers. And, to be frank, some of his curses seemed a wee bit too creative to be impulsive. There had definitely been some workshopping involved, I think.

There were several lessons to be learned. Firstly, never use the M6 to get to gigs – even if it means paragliding. Secondly, always run background checks on the medical records of everyone who books you. And thirdly, if you are going to bravely battle Tourette's and brazenly run your own comedy gig, don't stand right in front of the stage and throw verbal grenades at every other punch line.

It would be like inviting Christopher Hitchens to a Bible study. A *promoter*, with *Tourette's!*

May was my fullest month for gigs – with more than one every three days. The month ended a lot better than it had started. I did low-paid gigs for Jamie Sutherland and Mike Newall, plus a church gig with Tony Vino that went pretty well and reaped fifty quid. Dad's *Braveheart*-style pep-talk had made a deep psychological impact, and had allowed me to relax about the need to make money.

Ironically, what followed was the first month in which I made a profit. In all, I broke the 100-quid barrier in earnings and felt like a millionaire.

Even going out of the Laughing Horse at the semi-final stage didn't really faze me. I put in a decent showing, but other people were just better on the night – none more so than a certain softly-spoken Geordie lass.

Competitions, I concluded, were not going to lead to instant success or riches. Nor, though, did I need them to. What counted was to write every day and gig every night, and, most of all, to enjoy it.

The Full Moon gig was another belter, with Markus Birdman headlining and re-arranging the timbers. I'd managed to pick apart the scathing review, so that "Kind is not so much a talented performer, so much as a proponent of easy, formulaic comedy" became "Kind is a talented proponent of comedy." Everything, it seems, is redeemable.

And both on stage and in the air, the first strains of summer shone through.

***

It would be like going to a miner's strike wearing an "I love Thatcher" T-shirt – a *promoter*, with *Tourette's*...

June

I popped over to see Gran. I hadn't seen her in a while, and besides I wanted to borrow her Dizzee Rascal CD.

We sat and had a lovely chat. There's a wonderful rhythmic format to chatting with grandparents – a routine that never really changes. It doesn't matter what's been happening in the world – a chat with my Gran (or G-thang, as her neighbours had taken to calling her) always follows the same pattern.

Within a half-hour conversation with your Grandmother, you can always expect to drink more tea than your bladder can cope with; get offered a range of biscuits on a small plate – usually including a bourbon, a custard cream and one of those pink wafer things that nobody really likes but they keep making for just such an occasion; hear at least one story from the Blitz; get called by any name except the one that is actually yours, and have recounted to you at great length the latest goings-on in the post office – whether you show any interest in it or not.

But isn't that wonderful? There are voices of criticism that would castigate the older generation for being so "stuck in the past", and as we as a society grow more liberal, some views held by the old guard can seem a little narrow-minded or intolerant. But isn't it beautiful, nevertheless, that in such a rapidly changing world full of so much uncertainty, you can always find a stoic consistency in your Gran.

After I had heard the story about Margaret's arthritic bunions for probably the seventh time, and suggested twice in a minute that "coloured" wasn't the right term, my Gran wheeled out another of those stock phrases that is meat and drink for grandparents everywhere, but that is always touching to hear.

"I'm very proud of you, you know?"

"Thanks Gran."

"No, I'm serious. Very proud of you, I am. I was telling Margaret yesterday – bless her, her bunions are giving her real gip, did I tell you?"

"Eight times."

"Anyway, I was telling Margaret how proud I am of what you're doing with your comedy, and I told her how you travel round the country – I hope they pay for your travel, by the way – and that you've done competitions and you've been in the paper – it's still up on my wall, that article – and she asked if you'd been on TV and I said you hadn't but you were still building it up but that I was sure you would be – your Grandad would have loved to see you on TV – and she asked if you did a song between your stints because that's what they all used to do in the old days – I suppose things are different now, are they…?"

She's a wonderful lady, and she absolutely is proud of me. But then that is her job. When you get to that stage in life, there are two things that are incumbent upon you: (a) Never miss *Countdown*, and (b) Think that your grandchildren are the most talented people on earth.

Having seen me perform, it's rather moving to hear Gran say how proud she is of what I'm doing, but what alternative does she have? I'm hardly likely to hear, "Well, to be honest, I'm surprised you're making a living from anything, because, frankly, as a child, you were largely cretinous. We'd say, 'Go and get the yellow car', and you'd just go cross-eyed and drool from your massive moon-face. Frankly, I'm shocked you can use a knife and fork."

Danni had dumped me. It had been going pretty well for several weeks, but out of the blue she told me she was getting back with her ex. Ironically, I'd been reading a survey in one of her trashy magazines that put "good sense of humour" top of the list of traits that women look for in a potential suitor. Nowhere in the top ten did it mention "lunatic who used to be in the Parachute Regiment". It's almost as though those surveys are a load of tosh.

"I really like you, Andy, but Gary wants me back and I always dreamed of marrying a red beret."

My mumbled response was one of the worst comebacks of all time.

"Pfft! Me and my mates could have taken Arnhem bridge."

Disrespectful, anachronistic and pathetic – that's how I like to end all my conversations. And nobody has ever looked anything other than a buffoon after starting a sentence with "Pfft".

At least she was honest, I suppose. She did, however, use one of the phrases that oft gets spouted when two erstwhile companions re-unite. The "fallacy of justification", I call it:

"It's just that we have a history."

So what? What does that mean? How does that support your decision? You have a history – well done. So do Israel and Palestine, but they don't go to Nandos together.

It was probably for the best, though. I realized, to my growing apprehension and disquiet, that the only reason I had felt so relaxed with Danni, and felt so gutted at the split, was a Freudian one: she reminded me of a girl that I once knew; a girl from whom I believed – wrongly, as it turned out – I had unhooked all my affections.

Jess.

***

To tide me over between rejections and distract me from lucid daydreams of mortaring Gary at close range, Steve and Big Dave took me speed-dating.

It was down in Birmingham, so we piled into my Ford Focus and shouted "road trip" without really knowing why. Foaming at the mouth at the mere mention of the M6, we took a detour along the A51 through Lichfield (it's a good road, don't you worry about that). As a treat, I schooled the lads in Boat, Bike, Honk – an in-flight game that Mike Newall had told me about, and one of the many that comics use to while away the long hauls. In the same way that anyone who played Rugby at University will always have an archive of drinking games, comics build up a collection of driving games – both team and individual – to stop us going insane and axing people to death in lay-bys.

Boat, Bike, Honk is a very simple game, but also very more-ish. Basically, every time you see a car carrying a boat, you shout "Boat". If you shout it before anyone else in the car, and it is indeed a boat, you get one point. The same applies to "bike". The "honk" aspect of the game comes into play when you see a VW camper-van – you get three points for this. If, however, you shout "honk", but the camper-van turns out to be a different make, you lose three points and the psychological battle. The downside of the game is that, once you immerse yourself in it, it becomes almost impossible to stop, and you can find yourself walking through Halfords shouting like a mentalist.

The equivalent would be Stevie Wonder applying to be a tennis umpire. *A promoter*, with *Tourette's*?!?!

Steve and Dave both took to Boat, Bike, Honk very quickly, which was poorly thought out on my part, since the speed-dating took place at Brindley Place, overlooking the Birmingham canal. It led to a scenario whereby, every couple of minutes, one of us would shout "Boat!" and a handful of ladies would recoil.

Incidentally, in case you were wondering how I could possibly still have any kind of tie to Steve after the preceding nine chapters, by this stage of our friendship I *had* actually figured out that taking Steve along anywhere was usually a massive error and would lead inexorably to some major fiasco – either involving a near-death experience on stage or some kind of restraining order off it. Still, he was my best friend and, outside of him and Dave, my entire social circle was pixellated by Rockstar Games. You only needed to look at my Myspace page and observe that all my "top friends" were musicians that I'd never actually met to understand why Steve was still second in command.

I should say – indeed, I want to – that there is a lot more to Steve, and to our friendship, than the pages of this story might allude to. Yes, he vomits over vulnerable women; yes, he laughs when I fail; yes, he plays chicken with violent gangs of hooligans; no, he won't thank me for passing on this information to the wider public. But none of those things tell the whole story, and if I were to incorporate all of the times his friendship had made a positive influence on my life, this book would be at least two or three pages longer.

Steve is, in fact, a friend on merit, and whilst I have portrayed him as a boorish oaf, there is also a wisdom, a sensitivity and a loyalty to him that kept me sane through those formative months of my career. When I was angry and needed to rant, he listened; when I needed petrol money and was embarrassed to ask my parents, he lent me £20; when I felt forlorn and diced with quitting, he said "stick with it". A rounded picture doesn't always make for an exciting narrative, but it does Steve no justice whatsoever to portray him solely as a drunken loon. He is very much that, but also a lot more. And you will find, when we get to August, that the good far outweighs the bad.

So, speed-dating. Dave was already in a happy, stable relationship and so "wouldn't be trying", but just thought it might be a laugh. It wasn't.

Speed-dating is like rubbish counselling. You have three minutes to convince the person opposite that you're not incredibly lonely, even though the very fact that you're there suggests, quite strongly, that you're incredibly lonely. Oh, everyone says, "I'm just here for a bit of a laugh", but nobody laughs the next day when they check online and discover that, even among speeddaters, nobody wants to come near their face.

I'm cynical about the event of speed-dating, rather than the people who try it. I just found the whole thing a bit depressing. The whole idea of formatting and regimenting the concept of courtship just strikes me as a bit Orwelly. (Half-way through the evening, the tannoy announced that we'd just won a great victory over Eurasia, and we all cheered.)

The main bone of contention I have is that you end up getting drawn into the shallow points-scoring system. I met nine young ladies, all of them beautiful people in their own right, each of them possessing attractive qualities. And yet we were encouraged to make notes on our cards about the positive and negative aspects of the person facing us. And so, like a blind sheep, I noted down things like "left ear slightly too big", or "talks like a pirate", or "looks a bit stabby". Surely, the key to finding a partner in life is in the finding of beauty, not of fault?

In an odd twist of fate, one of the girls had, it transpired, seen me at a Spiky Mike gig.

"Were you the guy who does that stuff on *Ready, Steady, Cook?*"

"Yeah, that was me – what did you think?"

"......"

I noted down "no sense of humour" and waited for the three-minute bell.

The only positive was sitting next to Steve and Dave. After the first three of four bouts, you get bored of asking the same questions and start free-styling a little. I guffawed out loud during round five when I overheard Steve ask one girl who her favourite racist was – and just as much when Dave told a blonde girl, straight-faced, that he was a professional ghost. It may be the reason none of us got any follow-up. But then again, "we only went for a laugh". Yes, that's it – just a laugh.

We spent the return journey playing Boat, Bike, Honk, Hasidic Jew

– a slight variation on the original game where the new addition counted as ten points. As with speed-dating, we were all losers.

***

Singledom aside, life was looking moderately rosy. I was on a roll, comedy-wise, and paid gigs were being flown in and air-dropped left, right and centre. I had the privilege in June of working with acts such as Gareth Richards, Tim Vine, Mick Ferry and Ben Norris. I was learning something at every gig, and gagging alongside bigger names forced me to raise my own game. Neil "Spider" Smith even asked me to headline the Comedy Balloon. It was the first time I'd ever closed a show, and also the first time I'd done twenty minutes for a proper comedy night. It was a small, tight-knit crowd, but they were appreciative throughout and I came away feeling I'd done a workman-like job.

"Good to get that first twenty minutes out of the way. You'll grow into it the more you do. Good work," was Spider's complimentary but sparing feedback.

The cogs were still turning relatively slowly, but they were indubitably turning. My writing was getting tighter, my stage presence was getting stronger, and my improved bank balance meant I was crying less. After speed-failing in Birmingham, I jaunted back down to the second city for two gigs in three days.

The first was something of a pilgrimage, to The Bear in Bearwood. It was the gig that Frank Skinner set up in his early days as a stand-up during the late eighties, and there was a strong sense of comedic legacy hanging in the air.

Frank Skinner is my all-time comedy hero, having grown up obsessed by *Fantasy Football League* and, later, his live stand-up. His video *Live in Birmingham* remains the single funniest thing I've ever seen, and a bruised and battered VHS copy still graces the shelf in my study. From time to time, in a pique of nostalgia, I dust off the video recorder, sit back with a cup of tea and remember why I wanted to be a comedian. I recall watching it for the first time back in 1998 with my mate, Scott – tears rolling down our faces and hands clasping our sides as we struggled to breathe through the onslaught.

"I'd love to do a gig with Frank Skinner," I said to Scott, dreamily. It's a dream I still have.

In my experience, Brummies, next to Scousers and people with no inner ear, are the most difficult people group to amuse. This is just my experience, of course, and is possibly different from the majority of comedians. But trying to unpack a comedy routine in front of a Birmingham crowd has felt, at times, like wading uphill through muddy treacle – or something less idiomatically confused. The memory of Cheeky Monkey was still fresh in my mind as I found my way into the upstairs room. The crowd at The Bear were all seated around large round tables, and had decided to congregate predominantly towards the back of the room. My heart sank a little. I'd learned by this stage of my career, that disparate audience members aren't conducive to high laughter levels. Crowd members are like pieces of coal in a barbeque – separate them too much and they lose their warmth.

It was a tough gig, by all accounts. But comedians are confidence players, and good gigs tend to beget good gigs. I'd been on fine form and was in ebullient mood comedically. My cause was helped by compère Andy White, who decided to run a joke competition at the break to make the audience feel more involved and engaged.

"Finish this joke: 'Doctor, Doctor, I've lost my testicles…' And the winner gets two tickets for the next show."

Unable to play Boat, Bike, Honk in the upstairs room, I decided to pitch a couple of entries into the mix. I ended up winning the competition, with: "Regrettably, I'm a Doctor of literature and not of medicine, and am therefore not in a position to make a suitable diagnosis."

"It's somewhat auspicious," proclaimed Andy, "that that joke got the best response – because it was written by your next act. Welcome to the stage, Andy Kind!"

Getting my first laugh for free, before I'd even taken to the stage, made going on a lot easier than it might have been, and, though my set was still a bit like punching underwater, the smiles on the faces of the crowd were wider when I left the stage than when I walked on.

"Alroyte Bab!" one lady said – which I think means "Well done."

It was in this vein of confidence and good form/fortune, that I approached my first weekend gig at a proper bespoke comedy club: The Glee Club, Birmingham.

Each major city in the country – with a handful of notable exceptions – has a major comedy club. Newcastle has The Hyena, Nottingham has Just the Tonic, Leeds has The Hi-Fi and so on. These clubs, along with the Comedy Store and Jongleurs, make up the Premier League of comedy. They run predominantly at weekends, and they all tend to pack out with several hundred people at every show. My biggest crowd so far had been no more than 100, and I was about to see that quadruple.

Getting an open-spot or "try-out" at The Glee within my first year of doing stand-up is the equivalent of a Stafford Rangers player getting a trial at Aston Villa. The ideal process with these big clubs is that you do a couple of open-spot trials for them, after which they invite you to do a paid middle spot, followed by a paid opening slot and so on and so forth.

I certainly felt ready, and, my nine pre-gig toilet trips notwithstanding, I was confident of stepping up to the plate and knocking one out of the park. Strutting into The Glee, I very quickly learned that there was a divergent mentality to some of the smaller gigs I'd played.

I presented myself to the venue manager. "Hello, I'm Andy – I'm doing the middle spot."

"No, you're doing the open-spot. Follow me."

I was met with a cursory brusqueness that I wasn't used to and didn't appreciate. The venue manager, who refused to call me anything other than "open-spot" all night, took me through the back corridors of the building towards the Green Room. As we rounded one corner, I came face-to-face with a very well-known TV comic. I've changed his name to avoid conflict.

"Open-spot, this is Sean, he's doing the opener. Sean, this is open-spot – he's doing the open-spot."

"Hi, Sean, nice to meet you. How are you?"

"Don't speak to me like we're mates. I can't get you any TV work."

"I was just saying hello…"

"I hate ****ing open-spots – always trying to schmooze their way in. Look mate, I'm sure you're a good guy, but I don't want to be friends." Sean walked off to the bar.

Maybe he was just having a bad day, but it was just a hello – I wasn't asking to spend Christmas with his parents.

"Well, you asked for that," whispered the stage manager. "Come on, I'll introduce you to the others."

Actually, is there any chance I could get back in my car and drive away very fast?

Entering the Green Room, I thought I must have walked through a TV screen. Sitting around on raggedy sofas, chatting gently, were Milton Jones, Adam Bloom and Patrick Monahan. They all looked up from their conversation.

All the words I'd learned in the previous twenty-five years suddenly decided that now would be a good time to go on strike and refuse to work. I'm being completely truthful here – the only word I could remember was "*Bonjour*" (which is bizarre in itself, given that the French are usually the first to go on strike).

A look of slight confusion passed over the faces of Milton Jones and Adam Bloom, but Monahan leapt to his feet excitedly.

"Hey, *bonjour!*" he said, coming over to embrace me. "Are you French, then?"

"Er… no," I replied sheepishly. ("No" had clearly cracked first and, leaving the other hundred thousand words parading around with placards, had graciously come back to work.)

I'm so glad Pat Monahan was there to break the tension, because otherwise I might have sat there all evening in silence, while the other comics wondered why a nervous-looking French bloke had turned up.

Fortunately, Monahan *was* there. Pat is one of the most popular comedians around – both on and off stage. Not only is he a whirlwind of restless energy in front of a crowd, but he is the most genuinely warm, engaging comic behind the scenes. He could tell I was nervous, and went out of his way to make me feel welcomed and included in the conversation with the big boys. Adam Bloom and Milton Jones, it needs to be said, were also a delight, and spoke to me like a human being, and not like some youthful chancer trying to take their crown.

I mentioned that I'd not really done a big weekend club before, and they tried to allay my fears by saying things like "It's just the same as any other club, just with more faces to please", and "A joke in a small club that gets a laugh will still get a laugh in a bigger club."

Their advisory words did indeed allay my fears, although I didn't know at the time that they were lying. Well, not lying as such – just telling a half-truth. You see, laughter is contextual. A vicar unexpectedly telling a joke during a sermon will often get a big laugh – because it is incongruous with the rest of the talk (and as former Poet Laureate, Andrew Motion once stated, "Incongruity is humour"). That is the reason why plenty of vicars mistakenly think they are "using comedy" in their preaching. But a vicar trying to do that same joke to a comedy audience would likely be met with blank stares, because when an audience is expecting to be made to laugh, the bar is raised much higher.

Likewise, in a small comedy club where the line-up is largely made up of dreadful amateurs, a semi-competent act can get big laughs just by being one step ahead of that particular batch of comedians. It's all contextual.

But, and you can guess where this is going, a competent act – even a good one – can find him/herself playing to muted responses when sandwiched between comics who would be classed as exceptional.

Pat Monahan opened the show and made bantering look like a piece of cake, holding the 300-strong crowd in the palm of his hand. Then Sean went on and ripped it, too.

If that's him during a rough patch, I'd hate to see what he's like when he's on form.

After the break, Monahan again ad-libbed like a fiend, before bringing on Adam Bloom, who blew the roof off.

Waiting backstage, Milton told me another half-truth.

"They're nice and warm – you'll have a lovely gig."

Translation: You'll have a hard job following Adam.

What else can you say, though? A new act needs encouragement. It's morsels of hope like that that keep us going.

Milton Jones is a wonderful man. For someone so incredibly talented (he's widely regarded as one of the finest and most superlative wordsmiths in the world of comedy), he has a humility that I haven't seen in many acts – even people with a handful of gigs under their belt.

I'd heard Milton was a Christian, and I acknowledged that I was, as well, and that I felt called into comedy.

"Well, if that's true, then you've nothing to worry about – no matter how it goes tonight. Have a good 'un."

I was feeling ready now. Milton was right, it was in God's hands.

But then Sean, who I had consciously evaded at his behest, walked up behind me and whispered smarmily, "Enjoy this moment, mate. You're about to die on your hole."

"Ladies and gentlemen, Mr Andy Kind!"

Sean's comment had thrown me. It had pierced through the gaps in my armour, and instead of striding onto stage with bold confidence, I approached the mic with ominous foreboding.

"Hello!" I boomed.

"Hello!" the audience responded, in good voice. I rolled out my new joke.

"I was shopping in the Palisades earlier, buying some sexy lingerie for my girlfriend… when I bumped into someone who knows… that I haven't got one."

Slight pause.

Huge laugh.

Get in there! In your face, Sean. This will be fine…

"Do you watch *Ready, Steady, Cook?*"

I was off, into my stride and feeling good. I got about two minutes in and the audience were in raptures, laughing easily and even clapping some of the cleverer stuff. Then, from nowhere, someone shouted, "You look like Ross Kemp!"

"What's that, mate?"

"You look like Grant Mitchell, from *Eastenders*."

"No he doesn't," rang out another voice. "He looks like Phil Mitchell!"

"Duncan Goodhew," exclaimed another.

Without warning, the gig had turned from stand-up to an open discussion about which bald celebrity I most resembled.

"Sigourney Weaver," came another bid.

"Hang on, guys," I said, trying to maintain my calmness and facade of joviality. "I can't talk to you all at once."

"Yes you can," came the hammer blow. "That's what the microphone is for."

Huge laugh. Massive round of applause for the witty heckler.

I should have laughed. I should have rolled with it. But that is where experience comes in – experience I didn't have. I just stood there, rouging slightly, unable to think of a witty retort. The fourth wall had been broken, and it became obvious I wasn't a pro.

"Right, let's get back to my material, shall we?"

Too late. They had sensed fear. Toby Hadoke had told me, "You're in control until you let them think otherwise." Everyone now thought otherwise. I suddenly stood out like a massive, sore, amateur thumb. The crowd at this Premier League venue twigged that the manager was playing his Carling Cup side, and I failed to get a single laugh in the remaining three minutes or so of my routine – and believe me, when 400 people are staring at you, that is a long, long time.

As I shuffled back into the Green Room, I heard Pat pick up where he left off and the laughter levels shot up once more.

"Never mind, Andy," consoled Milton.

Sean just sat there, feet up on the table, chuckling.

"Nice one, mate – won't see you around, no doubt."

Crushed, shaken, mortified, disgruntled, distraught and wanting my Mummy, I slipped out of the venue unnoticed and trudged back to the car, passing Brindley Place on the way where, I noticed, there was another speed-dating event. Three minutes seems like nothing when you're chatting to a girl. It spans an eternity when you're talking into the potent silence of 400 Brummies.

Back to non-league football for me, then…

It may seem that I'm including a lot of failure in this story. Does it? Well, if it does, that's attributable to two major things. Firstly, there *was* a lot of failure in my first year.

You can read books by some top comics, where it's just a string of epic victories, culminating with a run at the Bloomsbury or their own Radio 4 series. But this book is designed to tell the story of the comedy everyman.

Stand-up provides a decent living, both for me and lots of people you've never seen on TV. But there are no short-cuts to success for 99 per cent of us. It's gig after gig and mile after mile. For every face you see on the television, there are hundreds who will never get near the small screen – either because they're not quite good enough, or they don't have the right look, or they want to keep some kind of artistic freedom. My hope is that this story provides an authentic account of the genuine struggles that anyone will find when trying to make a living out of something they love doing. (If it doesn't, well there's only two chapters left now anyway.)

Secondly, and more clinically, failure is more interesting to absorb. The most-watched clips on YouTube aren't "man gets given award for being top bloke" or "kitten escapes unharmed from tree". The clips that attract the mass hits are "snake eats rabbit whole" or "tramps fight to death".

It may well be trite and glib, but with comedy, practice does make perfect. Lots and lots and lots of practice. The best comedians on the circuit aren't those who have never fallen off the horse. They are those who were implacable about remounting, and about learning how not to fall quite so often.

Doing badly at The Glee was a kick in the teeth from a colossal shire horse. But it taught me that responding to heckles and interplay with an audience takes skill and assiduity. It led to me spending time writing heckle put-downs as well as jokes. It also gave me confidence the next time I performed to a large crowd – I'd done it before and knew what to expect.

Your first year is arguably about dispelling the fear. You encounter so many new and scary comic situations within the first twelve months, there's always something to unnerve you. But after a while, that fear dissipates. It never goes completely – you don't want it to – but you stop being a slave to it. And then, when you are master of your fear and not vice-versa – that's when you really start to progress as a comic.

July

Well, we've come this far together. Not far to go now, and I hope we can help each other over the line. I should warn you that something happens in August that you might not have predicted. It's not easy to write about, and it may not be easy to read. Just a heads-up really. For now, though, let's just try to enjoy July, shall we?

Once more into the breach…

"Hi Andy, it's Des Sharples here – I run Mirth on Monday in Chorlton."

"Hi, Des! I'd left a message on your phone last month about maybe getting a gig at your place."

"Yeah, sorry I didn't phone you back. Anyway, look – I'm going to be running a new competition called Anything for Laffs, and wondered if you'd like a spot in one of the heats?"

Not really.

"Well, to be honest, I've kind of decided not to do any more comps – I've not really fared that well in the others."

"Oh, I see. Well OK, but it's a local competition, there's only semis and then a final, and it's £1,000 for the winner."

Horlicks.

"Go on, then. When is the first semi?"

"It's tonight. We've had a drop-out, and Wayne Williams recommended you."

And so I enrolled in the last comedy competition I would ever enter: the inaugural Anything for Laffs new act competition.

Given that the climax of this book involves the final of this very competition, I won't bore you with swathes of minutiae detailing how I got through the semi-final. In a nutshell, Sarah Millican wasn't in it so I got through. In a delicious twist, it was Sarah who had pulled out of the heat, leaving me to step into the breach. Sarah had reached a stage of her career where her set was so good, not only had she won almost every comedy competition available to her, she was also being hotly tipped for non-comedy awards like the Turner Prize and Ryder Cup.

***

The competition on the night was hardly fierce. I won at a canter, with Victor finishing strongly in second. My highlight of the evening had been laughing at Victor before the start, as he sat in a darkened corner of the venue, shadow-boxing and listening to "Eye of the Tiger" on loop in his headphones.

Aside from Victor and me, it was reminiscent of the London Blitz. Several of the ten acts hadn't done more than a couple of gigs, and so one after another, they went on: bomb, bomb, bomb.

After nearly eleven months of this lark, my set was pretty secure, and I had enough in my locker to wrest some kind of positive response from an audience. Crucially, going on stage after four consecutive teenage debutants had churned out jokes solely on masturbation, onanism and touching yourself, I could have made cheese on toast and gurned silently, and I would have been out in front.

Some people might say that being the clear favourite to win made the act of winning something of a damp squib. You try telling that to the 2003 Rugby World Cup team.

I had expected to win, and my set had clearly been the most impressive, but when the results were read out at the end of the night, it felt like I'd broken through a wall.

"I'm in the final. Finally, I'm in a final! In your face, the world!"

Seeing runner-up Victor throw his Ipod across the room and

shout "Damn you, Rocky!" was worth the petrol money in itself.

As I collected up my coat and made my triumphal exit, a lady in her early twenties beckoned me over. She was leaning on the bar, looking like Shakira and instantly making me want to learn Spanish.

"Can I ask you a personal question?" she enquired.

"I think we'll have five kids – and I'd like to name them all after types of cheese."

The headiness of winning had elicited a ghastly, and frankly unacceptable, garishness to my social etiquette. I'd become everything I'd ever hated.

She smiled coyly, then said in a Welsh twang, "No, silly. I wanted to ask if you were a Christian?"

Eh?

What was occurring? Wracking my brains, I failed to recollect any moment from my set where I'd referenced faith in some way. My set was devoid of any swear-words or crudeness, but nobody had ever inferred Christ from that previously.

My heart leapt. This was amazing. Finally, after several years of following Jesus, and nigh on a year of trying to construct a comedy routine that stood out as different, someone had finally noticed God at work in my life. Already teetering on a self-satisfied brink, my brash confidence overflowed into outright smugness.

"I am, as it happens. How could you tell? Was it the righteousness you saw permeating the set?"

I smiled charmingly. She smiled back.

"No," she replied. "I can just tell you don't spend very much on clothing, so I thought that you might be. Bye…"

Des replaced her in my line of sight and caught the end of my sentence.

"… b******s…"

"What's wrong? I thought you were great tonight. See you at the final."

The final. It sank further and further in as I drove back to the Potteries. After countless occasions of losing my nerve, being outplayed and falling at the final hurdle, I had eventually reached the final of a meaningful competition – and I was potentially one solitary ten-minute set away from winning £1,000 and adorning my CV with a sparkly new credit.

I even rang my Mum as I drove back along the motorway, unable to stop the excitement from bubbling over.

"Mum, I did it – I made the BIKE!... Sorry, I made the final!"

"Oh, well done, Andrew. Are you hands-solo?"

"I'm hands-free, yeah. I'm just driving ba... HONK! I'm just on my way back now."

"Why do you keep shouting?"

"Just playing Boat, Bike, Honk on my own. You've got to keep your eye in."

"Well, I'm so happy for you, my boy. Shall I leave you out a big slab of cheese and a hot chocolate?"

"Yes please, Mum. See you soon. HASIDIC J...Oh wait, no, false alarm – that's minus ten, dammit."

The next day, I got an email from one of the young lads in the competition whose set revolved exclusively around his own private parts. In his email, he asked for some hints and tips on how to become a better comedian.

"It was a privilege to see someone with your experience show how it's done properly," he concluded.

A wry and slightly creepy smile traced its way across my face. This was weird and, at the same time, hugely exciting. Another comic was looking up to me. To me?! Almost overnight, I was no longer the bottom of the pile or last to get picked. I had been replaced as a fresher by a new season of green-horns.

Let's be honest: I was still, within the context of the national comedy circuit, a very new and very average act. I hadn't suddenly become Merlin or Dumbledore. But sometimes it's nice just to take stock of where you're at. I had been gigging less than a year, had dragged myself out of two near-fatal comedy crises, and was being viewed as a bench-marker by a younger comedian – albeit one so woefully inept that even the perennially supportive compère, Des Sharples, unplugged the mic after eight minutes of the poor lad's set and said, "I think we've had enough of that, thank you."

The date of the final was set for August, and before then it was pretty much business as usual. I spent the days writing and watching *Thundercats*; I spent the evenings travelling the country and trying to make people merry. It was just what I did. I was a comedian.

***

The highlight of July was being phoned out of the blue to be invited to host an eighties convention. I don't think there's anything more exciting in life than being invited to host an eighties convention – save for actually hosting the eighties convention – which is what I'd just been invited to do – hence I was excited.

Everyone, I believe, has a special pining for the decade in which they were born. There's something very comforting and escapist about wallowing in paraphernalia from the time of your conception and birth – from that period where everything seemed so simple and easy, and daily life was one long bounce on a space-hopper.

Different people have different impulses when they are reminded of the eighties. For some, their thoughts turn instantly to Thatcher's Britain – the miners' strike, the Falklands, and the suffering of an entire class of people; for others, it's about the music that grew out of that incumbency – The Specials, Madness etc. – and the gallant rebelliousness it championed. Further along the nostalgic spectrum you will find people who literally can't hear the phrase "the eighties" without singing something by Duran Duran, and for whom going to an eighties theme-night signifies the high-spot in their year/life.

These are all valid affiliates of the era. But I don't remember the Falklands or the miners' strike; I didn't listen to the New Romantics; I'd never heard of the Specials until my teens. Part of that is down to the fact that I was born in late December 1980, and was perhaps too young to be taking an interest in matters of politics and social unrest. But to me, there was something much more important than all of this; something that demanded the lion's share a decade; something that robustly and heroically flashes to the very front of my mind when anyone mentions the 1980s.

And that something is Optimus Prime.

Note to reader: I'm about to get really, really geeky. If you don't want to know the score, look away now.

There was nothing quite like *Transformers* for a pre-pubescent boy in those halcyon days. The "robots in disguise" graced our parents' screens with an enthralling narrative of moralistic tales, charting the progress of the intergalactic battle for supremacy between the righteous Autobots and those perennial bad prats, the Decepticons. More recently, I've learned that the original series contained intentional and non-too-subtle parallels with the Cold War. But you can over-complicate things, I think. For me, it will always be about a massive talking lorry pulverizing an evil pistol.

With so many of the half-remembered kids' shows from the eighties, a fresh, modern-day appraisal on YouTube leaves me feeling despondent and empty inside. The animation is sketchy, the voice-overs grate, the characters are one-dimensional and "unrelatable". Not with *Transformers*.

Even my second favourite icon from yesteryear, He-Man, exhibits massive flaws on re-evaluation. The main problem with the blond bombshell was that the production was so lazy. The cartoons were made to back up the line of children's toys that Mattel were bringing out. The fact that the whole programme was, as a consequence, just a massive marketing tool somewhat sullies the innocent memories I possess of a magical struggle between good and evil; it turns out it was more a corporate battle of supply and demand.

Anyway, the upshot of this sales ploy was that the artists working on the show had, ostensibly, no more than about six pieces of stock animation: He-Man running; He-Man punching; He-Man turning into He-man; Skeletor laughing like he'd been quoted happy; He-Man rearing up on Battlecat and then taking part in a Gay Pride parade. (OK, one of those is a lie, but it wouldn't be that surprising if you look at the outfit he wore.) If you take the time to watch more than one episode (and I think you've guessed, I have), what you find is pretty much the same six pieces of footage, but in a slightly different order.

Beyond that (and no, I haven't finished yet), it's completely incredible. Now, obviously, you might say, it's a cartoon featuring monsters and magic and so it's all incredible. Well, yes, except that once you set those parameters of fiction in place people will happily suspend their disbelief and watch away. But there still needs to be an internal consistency and logic to the narrative process – and such a process is lacking in He-Man.

At the start of each episode Skeletor devises a new, hair-brained scheme that he is certain will lead to He-Man's demise – having seemingly forgotten that He-Man is "the most powerful man in the universe", and therefore invulnerable to any attack from a man without a face. It's Skeletor's flippancy, and the level to which he misplaces his conviction, that galls the modern viewer (and when I say "modern viewer", I mean me – nobody else cares). Even on the odd occasion where He-Man is busy perving over Tee-la and Skeletor gets the upper hand, He-Man ultimately just hits him with a massive punch (stock animation number 2) and Skeletor flies off into the distance... until next time.

You don't get this sloppy logical implosion with *Transformers*. Watching it recently, what took me by surprise and delighted me in equal measure was the fact that sometimes the Decepticons won. Yes, good triumphed over evil eventually, but not without myriad defeats along the way. Sometimes the Autobots got completely trounced, Prime got shot to pieces and the situation seemed bleak and hopeless. (Of course you are going to lose the odd round when you're being attacked by a force of fighter jets and nuclear weapons, while your side consists of a Volkswagen Beetle, an articulated lorry and an FM radio.) And that is what made it such a classy show – because, although it was about tribes of autonomous robots from outer space, it was real. It reflected the reality of life – that good doesn't always win out; the good guys aren't always triumphant; often our hopes of justice coming through seem to lie, motionless, like a rusty heap of metal that used to be a shining red hero.

It's why the original volume of episodes is still so watchable; why the recent film was such a massive success, and why when I watch the 1986 animated film and Prime returns to the score of "You've Got the Touch", I still shed a tear.

Why is any of this important or relevant in the slightest? Well, quite simply, it's not, aside from the fact that for many years now my main two aims in life have been to write a book and to actually become Optimus Prime[10] – and this has the look of a happy medium. Having said that, the idea of being able to transform on a whim is relevant to the book, simply because it would make getting home from gigs a good deal simpler.

"Do you need a lift, Andy?"

"No thanks – I'm seconds away from morphing into a juggernaut, so I'll make my own way home."

I suppose I should try to tie *Transformers* to the narrative in some tenuous way. How about… "Optimus Prime. You know, that's

10   Or Grimlock, leader of the Dinobots.

a lot like Jesus."

Yes, that should do it.

***

The hosting part of the convention didn't actually involve much comedy. It was more a case of introducing a string of nostalgia to the stage – or "nostalgiacts", as they liked to be dubbed. From body-poppers to men with make-up to a dance-troupe all dressed as David Hasselhoff, if it had some kind of tie to the eighties, it was suitable for inclusion in the show.

The whole shebang lasted about five hours, and I ushered to the stage tribute acts including By Jovi (Yorkshire lookalike), Fleetwood Big Mac (tall bloke with high cholesterol), Silvery (featuring Debbie Harold) and, most bizarrely, OCDC.

OCDC are officially the only rock tribute act in Britain where all the band members suffer from obsessive compulsive behaviour. It made for a weird twenty minutes. They played one song repeatedly on loop, had to wash their hands between each reprise, and when some knickers were thrown playfully on stage, they picked them up and just tidied them away neatly in a drawer. Having witnessed the oddity of the proceedings, and the band's fidelity to their condition, I gave thanks that there wasn't a tribute act dedicated to The Specials.

Graunching towards the end of the show, I looked at my now-crumpled running order and saw that the last name on the list – the headliner – was a guy called Chesney Hawks (as opposed to Chesney Hawkes).

What's this going to be? A bloke in a bird costume singing "I Am the One and Only" and then eating a vole?

It was past 1 a.m. by this stage, and I was as tired as the idea to host an eighties convention in the mid noughties. Still, intro this

167

last tribute act and I could collect my cheque and head back to the future and back to the car.

"Ladies, gentlemen, and New Romantics who are neither one thing nor another... Are you ready for your headline act? Technically, this act should be part of a nineties convention, given that his one good song was released in that decade. I never rated the original – let's hope this guy is better than the person he's impersonating. Will you per-lease welcome to the stage, Chesney Hawks!"

The stage curtains opened, a familiar-looking man in a black leather jacket pushed his way onto the stage. Familiar, because I had just insulted the actual Chesney Hawkes. Time to leave.

The show manager accosted me as I sloped off stage. He caught the end of my sentence.

"... b******s!"

"You know that was Chesney Hawkes?!"

"I do now, yes. I'm sorry – it was spelt wrong on my running order. I thought it was going to be a man dressed as a hawk," I offered by way of excuse, sounding like a member of "The Very Specials".

Even now, several years later, thinking about that moment brings me out in a slight rash of cringe-worthiness. I exited the venue faster than mullets went out of fashion, cursing under my breath and feeling like Alan Partridge.

Compared to May, July was a quieter month gig-wise. It's the month where a lot of venues concentrate on Edinburgh previews, whereby comedians who are taking solo shows up to the festival in the ensuing month come along and road-test their material. It can mean that bog-standard comedy nights get held in abeyance until the autumn, but it also gives you, as a baby comic, the chance to see masters at work. One Monday evening, I hauled myself over to Derby along the A50 (it's a solid road, don't fear the reaper), to watch a double-header of Rhod Gilbert and Mark Watson. To see, up close, the formation of an hour-long narrative from two of Britain's very best stand-ups was akin to sitting next to a watchmaker as he meticulously constructs a timepiece. You can treat shows like that in one of two ways. You can either feel inspired, and drive home determined to reach that level of ability. Or you can heave a massively defeatist sigh of short-termism, and throw your gig diary in the bin. On returning home, I stayed up till 3 a.m., writing furiously and trying to perfect a Welsh accent.

I had my second attempt at a professional club that week, too, as Lee Martin from The Frog and Bucket invited me to do a ten-minute spot on a Thursday. I applied a Linford-Christie-style tunnel vision and didn't react to any heckles.

Ignore them and carry on.

It was enough to get me rebooked.

***

Victor had agreed to let me stay at his flat once more that night, and I amicably laughed off his promise to put bleach in my tea to stop me winning Anything for Laffs. I just stuck to water.

Walking back from The Frog to Victor's house through Ancoats, two of the most ridiculous episodes befell me in quick succession.

It was monsoon season as I navigated the back streets of north-central Manchester, with remnants of the industrial revolution looming round every corner. As the rain sheeted down, I skirted dilapidated factories, traversed disused tramlines, strode under railway bridges and slipped along cobbled streets where the rain made passage treacherous for a man who buys his shoes from Asda. In that part of the city, for whatever reason, the atmosphere is strikingly oppressive, and I was looking forward to the warmth and comfort of Victor's *chaise longue*. A couple of times I allowed my imagination to run away with me, and I envisaged turning a corner to find a pale-faced lady in Victorian dress beckoning me into a long-ruined mill. I'd helplessly follow her through the door, to find a horde of orphan children with sooty faces and flat cloth caps. One of them would say, "We've been dead for 200 years. Join us." And then they'd eat me.

This genuinely is how my mind works when he's left to his own devices.

Already on edge at the prospect of meeting ghost children from the past, my nerves were shredded further still when, on arriving at a main road, soaking by this point, a black BMW screeched to a halt yards from where I was standing. The windows were blacked out, but the bass from the stereo was tickling my eyes.

Am I about to be gunned down in a drive-by shooting?!

It was a hugely distressing prospect – I hadn't even made a controversial hip-hop record, let alone dissed anyone.

I mean, sure, I once said at a party that 50-cent's lyrics were vapid and uninspiring…

… But surely that can't have got back to him?

This genuinely is how my mind works when he thinks I'm about to be shot.

Then, in the most pleasantly surprising turnaround of all time, the driver's window wound down and I heard, to my utter bafflement, that the pumping bass banging out of the black Beamer was actually the 1986 Robert Palmer classic, "You Might as Well Face It, You're Addicted to Love".

There was still a chance I was going to get shot, but an eighties power ballad makes everything seem less scary.

"Excuse me, mate?" asked a man with a tiny head. "Do you know how to get to Old Trafford from here? I've come up from London for the match and have got a bit lost."

A United fan from London? Surely not.

"I don't, I'm afraid." I did.

"No worries. See ya…"

As I neared my destination and the promise of a bleach-traced cup of tea, the rain by now seeping into my marrow and putting pneumonia top of my list of fears – with Victorian spectres second and New Romantic drive-bys in third – the night took one final twist, both surreal and sad in equal measure.

Pacing soggily along an alley below Piccadilly Station, craving hot towels and whistling "Sledgehammer" by Peter Gabriel (because I, like everyone else, confuse him with Robert Palmer), a woman in black emerged abruptly from one of the ginnells. Being a butch man who remains cool under duress, I naturally screamed like a child.

The woman in black laughed playfully. Then she spoke.

"Are you looking for business, babe?" she enquired with a grin, running her ruby nails through her sodden, bleached hair.

I'd never met a prostitute; hadn't ever expected to, really. I was brought up in a leafy suburb, where the only people who walked the streets late at night were neighbourhood watch.

There are some moments in life that you can never be ready for, and which leave you feeling utterly helpless. Losing a grandparent for the first time at the age of eleven was one of those moments, as was rupturing my hernia two years later as I tried to take a penalty. Meeting this lady was another.

I can't pretend there was anything attractive about this woman. She was no older than thirty, but her face was weathered and a double-helping of mascara failed to hide what looked like a black eye. Her voice, heavily accented with a Lancashire twang, and so far from the silky tones of the harlots you sometimes see portrayed on TV, rasped and rattled out of her throat. She meant it to be seductive, but it felt like I was being chatted up by Jim Bowen.

She repeated her invitation. "Are you looking for business, babe?"

This was my chance. Here was a supreme opportunity to show

Faith in action, to engage with the shadowy side of society – a chance to be light in the darkness, to be salt of the earth. Here was I, a comedian – a modern-day prophet – a man with an advanced gifting for speaking out, for communicating truth. This was my chance to make a difference to the life of someone that life had spat out.

And what did I do? I turned into Wilson from *Dad's Army*. Instead of penetrating her suffering with my words, I became the most insipid, middle-class buffoon ever. And in response to being offered full sex by a broken lady of the night, I simply replied:

"Oh, I'm fine, thanks."

As though she had offered me a Polo!!

It got worse. On receiving my declination, her face dropped and she turned, rejected, and started click-clacking off along the cobbles in her heels. I still had a chance. I could still turn it around and bring redemption to the situation. I shouted after her:

"Best of luck with it all!"

What the hell was that?

This book, being based on a comedian's first year, is designed to make you, the reader, chuckle. And I really do hope that, so far, bits of it have made you laugh.

But laughter without truth is empty. Utterly. And, moreover, a comedian who doesn't bring hope through their comedy, in my opinion, fails to grasp what God intended laughter to be – a means of healing and restoring.

On a rain-drenched July evening in urban Manchester, comedy suddenly seemed so innocuous to me. The times I'd driven home from a gig, swearing, ranting, shedding a tear, now appeared so puerile and self-indulgent.

It's all very well entertaining a crowd of middle managers, before they return to their big-screen TVs and laminate flooring. But if when healing is really needed; if when you meet people who need serious blessing, you do nothing, what is the b***** point?

I plodded back to Victor's, my heart soaked through with remorse. It was one of the saddest moments of my life. I wanted to help her. I hate to see people in dire need. But being a humungous coward who hates confrontation, I took the path of least resistance and did nothing.

That night, as I failed to find warmth in my arctic sleeping bag, I implored God to wake me up from my spiritual sloth and hypocrisy. My career was going from strength to strength, but to gauge my encounter with the rain-addled prostitute in comedy terms, I'd died on my arse.

August

It was the weekend and I was bored.

I rang Tony Vino to ask how he was.

"Kindy, Kindy, Kindy – I'm at Greenbelt!"

"You're where?"

"Er, Greenbelt. How have you not heard of this?"

"What the heck is Green Belt?"

"It's only the best festival in the world ever. You should come down – it's awesome!"

I'd never heard of this "Green Belt" festival. It sounded like a gathering for people with a mild proficiency in Judo. Furthermore, I'd never been to a single summer festival – I try not to go anywhere that other people describe as "mental"; I simply don't see how that adjective could seem alluring. If I want to go somewhere "mental", I'll visit my Grandad.

My stance on festivals had always been, historically, that "nothing about it is as good as being at home": a tent is not as comfy as your own bed; food cooked on a stove is not as tasty or cheap as food cooked by your Mum; you can't get ravaged by a pack of wild dogs sitting at home. I'd always seen that as a fairly watertight argument for not uprooting myself for a weekend, just so I could get muddy, catch hypothermia and pretend I know what "having it large" means.

Feeling steadfast in my decision to shun this unknown festival for losers, I called Steve up to see if he wanted to have it large with a box-set and a bumper bag of cashews.

"Would love to, but I'm at Greenbelt. You should come down!"

Over the course of the next twenty minutes, I rang four or five "friends" with a view to "chillaxing" chez Kindy. I'm not kidding – they were all at Greenbelt. The whole world, it struck me, was converging on Cheltenham Racecourse – apart from me. I was half-expecting to switch on BBC News and have Huw Edwards say: "In a dramatic move, Tony Blair has postponed his trip to Iraq so he can go and watch Martyn Joseph on the main stage."

Fearing that I was somehow missing out on a well-kept secret, I assessed the predicament. On the one hand, I hated festivals and had managed to get through twenty-five years without setting foot inside one. The closest I'd come was the Westlands County Primary School summer fete in 1987. I held my Mum's hand, sampled various jams and came third in the three-legged race – it was mental.

On the other, larger hand, everyone I'd ever met or been in the same building as was either already at, or about to be at, Greenbelt. I could either bite the bullet, or I could spend the weekend visiting my Grandad and perusing his collection of bullets.

"I'll do it!" I said, leaping in the air with a clenched fist.

Maybe it wouldn't be that bad...

***

You know when you meet someone randomly, you get chatting, and within half an hour you feel like you've known them forever? Or when you're flicking through the many tiers of satellite channels and happen upon a show from the seventies or eighties that instantly enraptures you, delights you at its existence and yet frustrates you that it's taken so long to discover it? Welcome to Greenbelt!

Straddled across the August Bank Holiday weekend, and featuring music, comedy, an organic beer tent, workshops, an organic beer tent, countless food vans and a big tent that sells organic beer,

Greenbelt very quickly unlocked the door to my heart, settled a leather armchair by the fire and made itself comfortable. There's a song by Whitney Houston that goes: "I'm every woman… it's all in me." Well, if you changed the lyrics slightly to "I flippin' love Greenbelt", you would have a fair summation of how I was feeling as that first festival weekend unfolded.

All my friends were there, everyone was happy and laughing, and there was a very real sense of joy and peace. Without meaning to sound flippant or over-sentimental, it's exactly what I expect heaven to be like – but perhaps with less gortex.

I suddenly "got" what people mean when they wax lyrical about festivals, and I regretted not attending Westlands Summer Fete '88. It could have been so, so different.

The most striking, most exhilarating thing about Greenbelt was, and is, this: there were people like me there. Greenbelt is a Christian festival, and on paper very few concepts inspire less excitement than those two words next to one another. Given that I'd never felt the need to go to V or Glasto or Reading, I held little hope of being impressed by something with the word "Christian" in the title… unless it was "*American Psycho*, starring Christian Bale" – because that film is immense.

As a relative newcomer to the Christian subculture – having only made the decision to start following Him a few short years previously – and having had so little exposure to anything Christian other than the very small handful of believers I knew, my heart sang to find and chat to people who were not only normal, but engaging, inspiring, cool and relevant. I'd been worried I might be the only one!!!

It is possible to go to a Christian festival and simply witness the sort of happy-clappy, namby-pamby God-squad that spring to most people's mind when you mention religion; or, alternatively, the strict, pious religiosity that sits, straight-backed and surly, at the other end of the Christian spectrum. And if your views on Christianity are formed solely on what the media churns out, or from a few nightmarish Sunday school encounters as a child, then it is these two extremes that you will be familiar with. But there's the rub, you see – like anything in life, it is a spectrum.

There are, of course, people who fit with a stereotypical, pigeon-holed version of Christianity, but they are, I was starting to discover on this particular August Bank Holiday, very much the minority. Here I was, chugging pints of ale and munching on pie and mash, engaged in conversation with people who loved Jesus with their whole heart, but could also articulately discuss the career of Arsenal legend David Rocastle; who wouldn't just ask for an orange juice when you staggered to the bar; who wouldn't flinch if you dropped an f-bomb. In short, I wasn't witnessing Sunday morning religion. I was witnessing Christianity in its many shades and colours. It was rich, bold, contentious, scary, enthralling: it was real.

I chatted to a lady who had been chased across the Cambodian border for smuggling Bibles. I clinked glasses with a bloke who had been a bouncer and gang-leader and who met Jesus in a prison cell. I sat sipping whisky with a couple who sold everything they owned to open a homeless shelter, but who wore the biggest smiles of anyone I've ever met. I met a whole stack of amazing people, including a pretty Sussex girl named Becca who...no, that story will have to wait.

As a Christian, it's often easy to forget the joy and the love you experienced "the day you first believed". Life can get in the way, and the world can convince you that God is nothing more than a good-luck charm or a crutch. I've been to Greenbelt every year since that first occasion, and each time it reminds me precisely why I started following Christ, and precisely Who it is that I do follow. Keep your Sunday mornings. Keep your pews and your religious paraphernalia. Give me Greenbelt.

The Greenbelt weekend set me up nicely for what was set to be the biggest moment of my comedy career to date: Anything for Laffs – The Final.

***

The week leading up to the Final, the Manchester comedy forum was buzzing with excitement, and people were taking bets on who might take the title. I'd been listed as "evens" with Victor at 2/1. Being favourite is flattering, but also means there is more to lose if you aren't crowned champ.

BBC Radio Stoke had caught wind of the event, and invited me onto the breakfast show, to talk about my first year in comedy and how this was the pinnacle and culmination of a lot of gigs and a lot of hard work. The local paper declined to take up the story.

The day of the Final dawned, and I was up with the larks. I failed to sleep past 6 a.m., and resolved to pace up and down the garden in the morning dew, repeating my set into a Royal Doulton figurine of a ballet dancer (the carrot I used before the gig in Bath had long since been eaten). The summer air was bracing and fresh as I paced up and down the lawn, interacting with petunias and waiting for laughs from garden gnomes with fishing-rods.

Dad interrupted my flow at about 7.30 a.m. to bring me a stack of bacon sandwiches.

"Well done, son."

"Any chance I can have them a bit juicier?"

"They are. Well done on getting to the Final."

He was once more ensconced within the warm house before I had a chance to respond.

Steve had hand-made some T-shirts especially for the occasion, which read "Andy Kind should win: all the others are racist." Steve had mellowed a lot over the last couple of months – due, in no small measure, to his new girlfriend (and future wife), Erin. She possesses elf-like beauty and grace, and is nine years Steve's junior. I wondered initially whether Erin really was his girlfriend, or whether I was privy to a very relaxed hostage situation. However, they both seemed very much in love, and the security had released Steve to be positively effusive about my abilities and chances of success.

"You're gonna win it, Andy. This is your time. We'll pack it out with friendly faces, too – I've got friends."

Hearing a Northern Irish bloke tell you he's got friends isn't always the most reassuring thing to hear, but in this case it brought added comfort.

Gran tottered round to wish me luck, and handed me a signed photo:

"Best of luck with the comedy – Dizzee Rascal."

There wasn't time to delve into that particular story, so I said thanks and continued my preparation.

I had planned every breath, every nuance. I wanted my set to be pitch-perfect. I wanted the sum total of twelve months' hard graft to be displayed in this ten-minute performance. I knew where to look during which punch line, where to stand and how to modulate my voice.

I had trained for this. All those miles of motorway; all those notepads of half-soaked comedy ideas; all those little imperfections I'd ironed out, and all the mistakes I'd made and learned from.

I was ready.

The show was due to start at 8.30 p.m., and the clock in the hall seemed to tick louder and louder throughout the day, tolling for me. Steve arrived to pick me up just before six. The idea was to get there early, scope out the venue, get something to eat, run through the set again, and then try to relax.

"I'll just double-check the postcode online, Steve. Give me five minutes."

Logging on, I couldn't resist one last peep at Facebook while the AA route-finder was powering up, to check for any last-minute messages of support. Facebook is ideal for two things, and one of them is this sort of perpetual ego-grooming. The other is the reason I think most of us join Facebook after we leave school: to play that game of "Who got fat?"

"Ah, Laura Smith – dumped me in fourth year, now she's a heifer: 1–1."

Scrolling down the news feed, there were a few oblique references to the night from friends planning to go along. Smithers was in chest-pumpingly defiant mood about his chances, while Steven Woods (the trumping genius who came to the Full Moon gig) posted to say he'd heard the radio interview, thought I was a funny guy and wished me all the best. A gentle trickle of warm adrenaline started to drip its way into my veins. I was starting to tingle with excitement.

Then my eyes fixed on something that changed everything.

Half-way down the home-page, next to a thumbnail of a pretty girl with dimples on her face, I read the following:

"Jess is… battling the cancer as best she can."

And my world imploded.

***

When I was eighteen years old and just about to start my A-Levels, I started going out with a girl in my year called Jess. These days, if an eighteen-year-old girl approaches me, it's usually to see if I have a spare Werther's Original, or for help with some French homework.

Jess was gorgeous. She was the sort of girl you couldn't talk about without stretching out a hand and looking into the distance. A real Shakespearian beauty.

We'd been going out for roughly three weeks, and we'd just been for a romantic fish-and-chip supper. Now, before you start criticizing my chivalry, bear in mind that I paid for her portion *and* threw in a couple of pickled eggs as a nice treat. Dairy and vinegar – what can go wrong?

We got back to my car. (That's right, ladies – I paid for her meal and drove her home afterwards! And I didn't ask for much petrol money.) As I fastened my seatbelt, Jess turned to me and said, "Andy, I love you."

That was the first time anyone who hadn't given birth to me had told me that, and it was amazing to hear. And so, naturally, I returned the compliment.

"I love you, too."

On this ever-cooling cosmic pebble of ours, can there be anything more wonderful than two people saying "I love you" to one another?

Yes, I think so. I think it's more wonderful when two people say it and mean it. The problem was that… I didn't.

I wasn't in love with Jess. I would have been happy if I had been. I thought she was lovely. I thought she was loveable. But I wasn't in love with her. So why did I tell her I was?!

Because, as we have discovered, I'm a humungous coward who hates confrontation and sidles, aimlessly, along the path of least resistance. And it's easier to lie.

That statement – "I love you" – can only elicit three possible outcomes. Unlike when somebody asks you for your views on monkeys or cheese, where there is an abundance of varied and colourful responses, when someone tells you they love you, you are faced with a mere trio of choices. Firstly, you can smile politely, say, "I wish I felt the same, lass", and then watch as her face dissolves into a mess of different fluids. Secondly, you can distract her by feigning a massive stroke or heart-attack, then, when she runs to phone for an ambulance, drive off at high speed and hide in the woods for a year.

Or you can just say it back.

It may seem like a perfectly innocent thing to do in that situation – it certainly did to me. Jess was glowing on the journey home, talking about the future and babies and how sweet we were as a couple. So, on the surface, you might say, my words were harmless.

But I had lied.

I had told a lie to someone who loved me – a lie that misled her, that distorted reality. I had used words to deceive.

From that point on, our relationship would be based on an untruth.

It was the first lie I ever told Jess. But it wouldn't be the last.

After our A-Levels, we both went to University. I went to Warwick, while Jess was at Birmingham, so we saw each other most weeks, owing to the close proximity. This was great news. I really wanted our relationship to work. No, I didn't love her – yet – but it would probably happen eventually. I had no thought of breaking up.

University isn't the best place to find moral stability. I invested most of my energy into thinking up novel and exciting reasons why I couldn't hand in coursework. All of them fictional, they ranged in severity from having one of my parents die to being attacked by a macaque whilst sleeping. Again, it's easier – and often more fun – to lie.

I somehow managed to fit Jess in between the creative avoidance of study and the copious quantities of beer. But even though I saw Jess every week, I saw other pretty ladies every day. Pretty ladies who fancied me, and had their own rooms on campus.

One such lady was called Natasha – a Cornish girl from my French class. She was fit as!

Jess had been my best friend through Sixth Form, and we were seen as practically inseparable by our friends and some of the nosier teachers. But now we were separate, and Natasha stepped into that alpha female role that Jess had made her own. We studied together, went dancing together, had the same friends, knew the same local haunts. While Jess was only thirty miles away, she wasn't a Warwick student. She wasn't one of us.

The betrayal began at a traffic-light disco.

Call it a desperate need for affirmation. Call it over-inflated ego. Call it insecurity. Whatever you call it, there is no excuse.

Natasha was ostensibly the most fervent advocate of this traffic-light disco. Whilst many had come in delicate tones of green, she was dressed as Robin Hood.

Kissing her was only a matter of time, as Horatio had been telling me for several weeks. I was drunk, emotionally weak and hypnotized by eighties classics. Natasha made her move.

I protested initially, on the basis that I was wearing red.

"I'm colour blind!" she smirked.

Natasha told me I had to kiss her because otherwise I'd hurt her feelings. I don't like to hurt people's feelings, as we've already discussed. So I kissed her. Lots.

The next day I woke up feeling sick. Now, I often woke up feeling sick — snakebite and black does that — but this was different. I knew I was going to have to tell Jess. I couldn't do something like that and not confess it... could I?

Well, why not, actually? It would only break her heart if I told her. Plus, nobody who knew was going to grass me up, and what happened with Natasha didn't even change how I felt about Jess — I still wanted her as my girlfriend.

Having rationalized it, I decided to keep my mouth shut. I also decided to see Natasha again — in normal clothes and in none. In addition, I ventured to see who else I could snare with my charms. I was the smooth operator — attached but not tied down. During one week in my second term, I had six different girls sleep in my bed. None of them was Jess.

Let me run you through my logic at the time, just so you know how idiotic a man can be when he's fuelled by lust…

I really wanted to love Jess. I really wanted not to want to cheat. And I was certain that, eventually, I would only want Jess. I saw it as having met the right girl at the wrong time, and by sleeping around and playing the field I was simply getting it all out of my system, so that when Jess and I finally got married, I would have sown enough wild oats to settle down.

What a load of utter crap…

What I was doing – all I was doing – was misusing and violating the trust of someone whose trust was in me. It all dated back to that day when she said she loved me and I said it back. The first time you lie to someone, and realize how easy it is, it becomes a habit. For me, the habit lasted for nearly four years.

Eventually, in my final year of University, after I had been away to France and perpetuated the sham-like cloak-and-dagger relationship with Jess across the English Channel, someone finally told me to stop.

My friend Ali found out what I'd been doing and confronted me in the Students' Union during a seventies night in which I'd gone dressed, appropriately, as a pimp.

"I can't believe what you're doing. You have to tell Jess!"

"How can I?!"

"Because there is nothing that is hidden that won't be revealed. She is going to find out eventually. Now unclamp yourself from whoever you're with tonight, take what shred of decency you have left, and go and tell her!"

So I did. It was remarkable how easily I was challenged on it. I changed out of my pimp outfit, drank some strong coffee, and I went to Birmingham.

And, watching Jess' face turn from one of love and safety to one of confusion and torment, I told her everything. Everything.

At first she laughed, thinking it was a joke. Then she interrogated, wanting more detail. Then she started crying. Not crying like you would at the end of a movie with Matt Damon. Crying like you would at the funeral of your best friend – which, in effect, was what it was.

Then she threw me out.

As I stumbled through the doorway, I tried to utter a feeble "I'm sorry", but the door slammed. And, shockingly, mark this: I wasn't sorry. I just said what I thought I needed to say, but, in reality, I was only sorry that I couldn't have my cake and eat it. I had lied yet again.

Before I could get back to the car, the door re-opened. I turned, to see a human being who had had her future pulled from beneath her feet. She said one more thing to me before closing the door for the final time. It sounded like "I never want to see you again."

But I can't be sure – she was crying too much.

That had been the last time I'd seen Jess.

She had accepted my Facebook friend request only a few weeks ago, but I'd not found the time, as yet, to check her profile. And now I was reading this.

Facebook updates tend to be a little more urbane than that, usually. I'm more accustomed to reading "Dave is… not a gay, despite all the rumours", or "Sarah is… in need of a big poo, but can't 'cos she's at work."

To have not seen her in years, and now to be confronted with this fact, broke me in two. Somewhere in my soul a dam burst and, in an instant, all of the guilt, all of the grief, came flooding back –

whooshing through my body and pouring out through my eyes.

I called Lucy – the only one of Jess' friends who would still talk to me. She confirmed what I hoped wasn't true. Jess was dying.

I don't have the space or the vocabulary to dissect all the emotions that emerged from me at this point. I felt fear like I'd never felt before a gig; pain like I'd never felt after bombing; anguish like I'd never felt after being heckled. Those things registered now as tiny tremors on an emotional seismograph that was overloading and ready to malfunction.

In the mêlée of confusion and chest-pounding distress, I knew one thing: I needed to say sorry. And this time, I needed to mean it.

***

"Steve, we're not going to the Final."
    "What are you talking about?"
    "Jess is dying. We're going to Bath."
    Steve looked me flat in the face.
    "We'll need more petrol, then – and some pork pies."
    In tacit consent, he started the engine.

So off we went – south instead of north, full of sorrow rather than joy. The humungous coward who hates confrontation had swerved off the path of least resistance and onto the M6 south.

Comedy was my childhood sweetheart. Being a comedian was all I ever wanted to do for a living – the job I dreamt about, craved, pined for. Winning Anything for Laffs and a cheque for £1,000 would claw that dream ever closer to being a reality.

But laughter without truth is empty.

Jess was working as a physiotherapist down in Bath – the site of my first ever gig. I spent the whole journey down to the West

Country in near-silence, mewing softly and intermittently. Steve, like a massive trooper, just drove and drove. I texted Des with my apologies and said I'd call him in the morning. I texted Victor, too:

"Pulling out. Win it. Have a good 'un."

"It's for the best," was the terse reply.

We took the same road into Bath as I had almost one year previously, even passing the Porter Cellar Bar on our way. Steve briefly turned on the radio, which I turned off almost instantaneously – catching a few fuzzy strains of The Smiths' "There is a Light that Never Goes Out" before silence reclaimed the atmosphere.

"What if she's not in?" I said, the thought only just crossing my mind.

"We'll wait," said Steve stoically.

Lucy had given me Jess' postcode and we found the house easily enough. Light was streaming from a downstairs window. Steve parked up and punched me on the arm.

"Have a good 'un," he breathed.

I got out of the car, my legs turning comprehensively to jelly. I was shaking with fear. I must have looked like some hideous ventriloquist's dummy that had sprung to life and turned on his master.

As I walked up the garden path, I almost tripped on several implements strewn across my path, but the glow from the living-room window was enough to help me navigate safe passage to the porch.

Stepping on the mat, a security spotlight flashed on above my head, illuminating me in the darkness.

I paused, swallowed some sick, and rang the doorbell.

Standing there alone in a pool of light, I wracked my brains for clever things to say.

But when Jess opened the door, I just stared at her. And she stared back.

After what seemed like three or four days, but was more accurately no more than ten seconds, with heart pounding I finally spoke.

"Jess... I'm so sorry to hear... I'm so sorry that... Jess, I'm sorry."

Then she started crying. Then she threw me out.

The door slammed. Then I started crying too. Not crying like you would at the end of a movie with Matt Damon. Crying like you would at the funeral of your best friend – which, in effect, was what it was. For a few precious moments, I had looked into the eyes of the girl whose heart I had torn in two; the girl who had spread her dreams under my feet, for me to trample on with boots of lust and self-gratification; the girl who, in my mind, as it turned out, all subsequent girlfriends had been compared to, and to whom no other came close. A girl who might not make it to Christmas.

Before I could get back to the car, the door re-opened. I turned, to see a human being who had had her future pulled from beneath her feet. Standing there, the two of us weeping uncontrollably, I heard her say one more thing to me before closing the door for the final time.

It sounded like: "I forgive you."

But I can't be sure – she was crying too much.

As the door closed behind her, I slumped, helpless, to the floor – paralysed by grace. Steve had to carry me back to the car.

September

If this story only contained incidents from my first year in comedy, I would have to end it there. But, if you'll allow me, I'd like to stretch the parameters a couple of weeks into my second year.

Five weeks later, as leaves fell and chills set in, and as Victor still sent me regular texts about how he was spending his £1,000 worth of winnings, I saw another Facebook update that left me speechless. It simply read:

"Jess… is in remission and has been given the all clear."

It's amazing the minutiae you remember from key moments in your life. I remember seeing a tabby cat parade along next door's fence; I remember a lingering taste of bacon from the sandwich Dad had made me in his new George Foreman grill; I remember how the tears that rapidly filled my eyes obscured the computer screen, and how my commemorative David Rocastle shirt got wet from drying them. I remember all of that.

And then, if I remember rightly, I laughed.

Amen.

Thanks, acknowledgments and a historical note

I am deeply indebted to Monarch Books for commissioning this story. I've never been what you might call a "finisher". Indeed, of the many manuscript ideas that I have tucked away in various dwarves (that should read "drawers" - oh well, too late to change it now), this is, as yet, the only one I've managed to bring to completion.

There are plenty of people to thank. All of the people featured in this book, having been integral to my first year in comedy (and beyond), have my most sincere thanks for providing such rich tapestry. I should say that the passing of time renders it difficult to remember direct speech accurately. What I have tried to do, therefore, is to encapsulate the spirit of what each person said - and to represent the impact each person had on those twelve months. Some names have been changed; most haven't. Additionally, there are some fine fellows – Neil Reading, Dom Woodward and Paul Kerensa amongst others – who I really wanted to include in this story, but couldn't find space or time. Next time...

Big Thanks to the select group of people who read the sample chapters and offered encouragement and inspiration: Vino, Spider, Seany, Angel Beast, Don Gregory, Pete Ball, Tim Hill, Howard and Matt Bradley. Extremely grateful.

Steve – for being like a Bridge Over Troubled Waters, and for embodying true brotherhood.

To my awesome Mum and Dad, a HUGE thank you and much love, for making it all possible. This book does nothing to account for everything you have both done for Gemma and me.

Becca – this story marks the end of the night. With the next one, and with you, comes the dawn. (I just haven't met you yet.)

To Jess, if indeed that is your real name. Enough now...

And finally, and in all things, I give thanks to the King.
www.andykind.co.uk